IN THE RAYS OF LIGHT

LIVING THE QURAN
THROUGH
THE LIVING QURAN

I0263609

SŪRAH AL-WĀQIʿAH

THE IMPENDING REALITY

Written by Shaykh Muḥsin Qarāʾatī
Translated by Saleem Bhimji

Edited by Arifa Hudda

ISBN 978-1-927930-62-5

Commentary of Sūrah al-Wāqiʿah
A Translation from *Tafsīr-e Nūr*
Written by Shaykh Muḥsin Qarāʾatī

Translated by Saleem Bhimji
Edited by Arifa Hudda

Published by Islamic Publishing House

www.iph.ca · iph@iph.ca

Cover Design and Layout by Saleem Bhimji

Contents

Foreword by the Translator i

An Introduction to Sūrah al-Wāqiʿah 5
Specifics of this Chapter 6
Merits of Recitation 8

Part 1: The Great Event – Verses 1-6 11
Thinking Points 11
The Earth and the Mountains before the Resurrection 14
Take Away Messages 17

Part 2: Three Groups – Verses 7-16 19
Thinking Points 20
Take Away Messages 25

Part 3: Some Pleasures of Paradise – Verses 17-24 27
Thinking Points 28
Take Away Messages 28

Part 4: Barriers and Impediments – Verses 25-26 31
Thinking Points 31
Take Away Messages 34

Part 5: Those in Bliss – Verses 27-40 35
Thinking Points 36
Take Away Messages 40

Part 6: The Wretched People – Verses 41-48 41
Thinking Points 42
Comparison between the People of Heaven and Hell 43
Take Away Messages 48

Part 7: Everyone will be Brought Back – Verses 49-50 51
Thinking Points 51
Take Away Messages 52

Part 8: An Unbearable Punishment – Verses 51-56 55
Thinking Points 55
Take Away Messages 57

Part 9: The Proofs – Verses 57-60 59
Thinking Points 59

Take Away Messages 61

Part 10: Being Brought Back – Verses 61-62 63
Thinking Points 63
Take Away Messages 65

Part 11: Ever Thought About... – Verses 63-67 67
Thinking Points 67
Take Away Messages 69

Part 12: Think About Your Water – Verses 68-70 71
Thinking Points 71
Take Away Messages 74

Part 13: The Fire we Kindle – Verses 71-74 75
Thinking Points 75
Take Away Messages 77

Part 14: Oaths of Allah – Verses 75-76 79
Thinking Points 79
Take Away Messages 80

Part 15: The Noble Quran – Verses 77-80 81
Thinking Points 81
Take Away Messages 87

Part 16: How Can People Still Deny – Verses 81-82 89
Thinking Points 89
Take Away Messages 91

Part 17: The Reality of Death – Verses 83-87 93
Thinking Points 93
Take Away Messages 95

Part 18: Summary of Groups of People – Verses 88-96 97
Thinking Points 98
Take Away Messages 102

Conclusion by the Translator 105

Other Publications Available 109

Upcoming Publications 113

In the Name of Allah,

the All-Compassionate,

the All-Merciful

Foreword by the Translator

From the multitudes of commentaries *(tafāsīr)* that have been written by Muslim scholars over the past 12 centuries in their attempts to better understand the Quran and make it relevant to the lives of everyday Muslims, the present work of Shaykh Muḥsin Qarā'atī, *Tafsīr-e Nūr* – The Exegesis of Light, is a unique attempt to bring the Quran into the homes of all of humanity.

Although sometimes very brief in his explanation, Shaykh Muḥsin makes up for the brevity of the commentary by providing the reader with **Take Away Messages**. These detailed points guide the readers to key pieces of guidance on how to make the Quran relevant to their daily lives – thus, being able to *Live the Quran Through the Living Quran.*

We hope and pray that the translation and publication of this commentary serves to bridge the great divide which has existed within the Muslim community for generations and allows them to benefit from the beautiful teachings of the Noble Quran in their daily lives.

The initial project to translate *Tafsīr-e Nūr* into English was envisioned in early 2018 and was initially meant to strictly be a podcast rendition of the translation.

However, due to popular demand and the support of well-wishers around the world, we expanded the scope of this project to release the PDF of the commentary of each chapter of the Quran as we completed them.

With the advancement in Print-On-Demand services globally, we have taken it a step further and decided to release the translation of the commentary of each chapter in print version.

Most commentaries of the Quran are published with each volume consisting of hundreds of pages, and this often puts some people off from wanting to try and understand the Quran. It is our hope that by publishing the commentary of the Quran in the format we have chosen – that is, chapter by chapter – readers will be encouraged to pick up the exegesis of the chapter that interests them the most. In this way, over time, they will have read the commentary of the entire Quran, gaining inspiration from its teachings.

As we present this work to our readers, we are deeply grateful to all of those who have made it possible.

We extend our heartfelt thanks to our editor, Sr. Arifa Hudda, whose tireless dedication and expertise have been instrumental in bringing this project to fruition. For almost 25 years, Sr. Arifa has been a cornerstone of the Islamic Publishing House, guiding our publications with her keen insight and unwavering commitment to excellence. Her contribution to this work, as with all our publications, has been invaluable.

We would like to thank those donors who financially contributed towards the publishing of this book, as well as the other books in this series, and we ask you to recite a Sūrah al-Fātiḥa for their rewards and their dearly departed loved ones *(marhūmīn).*

We are also profoundly grateful to our well-wishers, whose generous support – in many ways – enabled us to undertake this ambitious project. Their belief in the importance of the Quran, and their commitment to fostering a deeper understanding of the Book of Allah within our community have been a constant source of inspiration and encouragement.

In closing, if you would like to support this project by sponsoring its publication, either individually or with your family, friends, and community members, choose a chapter of the Quran that you would like to see published, and contact us at iph@iph.ca for more information.

In conclusion, we pray to Allah ﷻ to accept the translation of this brief, yet unique look into Sūrah al-Wāqiʿah, and that we can spread the beautiful teachings of Allah ﷻ through *Living the Quran Through the Living Quran.*

Saleem Bhimji
Director *of the* Islamic Publishing House
18th of Dhul Ḥijjah, 1446 AH
14th June, 2025 CE
Richmond, B.C., Canada

سُورَةُ الوَاقِعَة

An Introduction to Sūrah al-Wāqiʿah

Sūrah al-Wāqiʿah is Chapter number 56 of the Quran, has ninety-six verses, and was revealed in the city of Mecca.

One of the names of the Day of Judgement is *'Wāqiʿah'* meaning 'an event which will transpire.' In the first verse of this chapter, we have been informed about this definite event that will transpire; therefore, this chapter was given the name *al-Wāqiʿah.*

Most of the verses of this chapter speak about the Resurrection and its conditions, and the events that will occur on that Day. This chapter also divides people into a few groups – namely those destined for Hell, and those going to Paradise. Regularly reciting and learning about this chapter will help keep a person from falling into heedlessness *(ghaflah).*

When ʿAbdullāh ibn Maṣʿūd, one of the companions of Prophet Muḥammad ﷺ, was on his death bed, ʿUthmān ibn al-ʿAffān, the third caliph, came to see him and asked him: "[From your life] what grieves you (the most), and what aspirations do you have?"

Ibn Maṣʿūd replied: "My past sins grieve me, while I look forward to the Mercy of Allah."

He was then asked by ʿUthmān: "Is there anything you want, that I can grant it to you?"

ʿAbdullāh ibn Maṣʿūd replied: "No thank you. When I was in need, you deprived me; so now that I am about to leave this world, what need would I have [from you]!?"

ʿUthmān then said: "So then permit me to give you something which you can then in turn pass on to your daughters to inherit from you."

To this, ʿAbdullāh answered: "They too do not need anything because I have taught my daughters something that [if they follow it] they will be needless. I have advised them to recite Sūrah al-Wāqiʿah, as I heard the Prophet say: 'Whosoever recites this chapter every night will never have poverty or loss affect them.'"[1]

Specifics of this Chapter

As one can tell from its name, the key theme of this chapter is a definite event: the Day of Resurrection – and some of the specifics surrounding that Day. As we will see, this is actually a constant theme repeated throughout its verses.

In general, we can divide the discussions found in this chapter into the following eight categories:

1. The preliminary signs to initiate the Day of Resurrection, and some of the frightful events that will take place.
2. Dividing humanity into various categories on the Day of Judgement – most notably:
    a. Companions of the Right Hand *(Aṣḥāb al-Yamīn).*
    b. Companions of the Left Hand *(Aṣḥāb al-Shimāl).*

---

[1] Ṭabrisī, Abū ʿAlī al-Faḍl al-, *Tafsīr Majmaʿ al-Bayān.*

   c. Those People Closest to Allah ﷻ *(Al-Muqarrabīn).*
3. A detailed discussion on the stations that the people closest to Allah ﷻ will enjoy, and some of their rewards.
4. A detailed discussion regarding the second category, the 'Companions of the Right Hand,' and some of the Divinely-granted gifts that they will be given.
5. An important discussion regarding the 'Companions of the Left Hand,' and some of the painful punishments they will be subjected to in Hell.
6. A mention of various proofs regarding:
   a. The Resurrection and its possibility based on the Ability and Power of Allah ﷻ.
   b. The creation of the human being from an insignificant drop of sperm.
   c. The manifestation of life in the plant kingdom.
   d. The descent of rain.
   e. The spreading of fire.

All of these are regarded as being signs pointing to Monotheism *(Tawḥīd).*

7. A clear representation of the state of a person at the time of death when the soul is leaving the body as they go from this world into the next – that world being the start of the Day of Resurrection.
8. A summary of the rewards given to true believers, as well as the punishments given to belligerent disbelievers.

In closing, there is a remembrance of the great Name, Allah ﷻ.

Merits of Recitation

There are numerous *aḥādīth* that speak about the rewards of reciting this chapter. For example, Prophet Muḥammad ﷺ is reported to have said: "It will be recorded that the person who recites Sūrah al-Wāqiʿah is not from among the spiritually-heedless individuals *(al-ghāfilīn)*."[2]

Such a reward will be given to those individuals who read and reflect on this chapter, as its contents should be enough to wake them up from their spiritual slumber of the life of this world.

Prophet Muḥammad ﷺ was once asked: "Why is it that the effects of old age have appeared on your blessed face so soon [while you are still 'young']?" To this, he replied: "[The following chapters of the Quran] have made me old before my time: Hūd, al-Wāqiʿah, al-Mursalāt, and ʿAmma Yatasāʾalūn (Sūrah al-Nabaʾ)."[3]

The reason why Prophet Muḥammad ﷺ made note of these four specific chapters of the Quran has something to do with the powerful tone that is used in them regarding the Resurrection and Day of Judgement, and the frightening events that will transpire from that Day forward – most notably, the retribution given to the guilty sinners who never

---

[2] *Tafsīr Majmaʿ al-Bayān*, Vol. 9, Pg. 212; Sayyid Hāshim al-Baḥrānī, *Al-Burhān fī Tafsīr al-Qurān*, Vol. 4, Pg. 273:

مَنْ قَرَأَ سُورَةَ الْوَاقِعَةِ كُتِبَ لَيْسَ مِنَ الْغَافِلِينَ.

[3] Shaykh Ṣadūq, *Al-Khiṣāl*, Vol. 1, Pg. 199, Ḥadīth 10:

شَيَّبَتْنِي هُودُ وَالْوَاقِعَةُ وَالْمُرْسَلَاتُ وَعَمَّ يَتَسَاءَلُونَ.

repented in the life of this world. It may also be due to the powerful, moving stories that are noted in these chapters about past generations, and the tests and tribulations they were subjected to; as well as the themes in these chapters to stand strongly and be resolved on the path of the truth.

In a final *ḥadīth* from Imam Jaʿfar al-Ṣādiq ﷺ, we read that: "A person who recites Sūrah al-Wāqiʿah every Thursday night (the night preceding the day of Friday), Allah will love them and will create love for that person in the hearts of the people. He will keep that person away from misfortune, poverty, helplessness, and calamities of this world. That person will be among the companions of the Commander of the Faithful (Imam ʿAlī ibn Abī Ṭālib ﷺ). This chapter is completely related to the Commander of the Faithful only and no one else."[4]

---

[4] Shaykh Ṣadūq, *Thawāb al-Aʿmāl wa ʿIqāb al-Aʿmāl*, Ḥadīth 1:
مَنْ قَرَأَ فِي كُلِّ لَيْلَةِ جُمُعَةٍ الْوَاقِعَةَ أَحَبَّهُ اللهُ وَأَحَبَّهُ إِلَى النَّاسِ أَجْمَعِينَ وَلَمْ يَرَ فِي الدُّنْيَا بُؤْسًا أَبَدًا وَلَا فَقْرًا وَلَا فَاقَةً وَلَا آفَةً مِنْ آفَاتِ الدُّنْيَا وَكَانَ مِنْ رُفَقَاءِ أَمِيرِ الْمُؤْمِنِينَ وَهٰذِهِ السُّورَةُ لِأَمِيرِ الْمُؤْمِنِينَ خَاصَّةً لَا يَشْرَكُهُ فِيهَا أَحَدٌ.

Part 1: The Great Event – Verses 1-6

بِسۡمِ ٱللَّهِ ٱلرَّحۡمَٰنِ ٱلرَّحِيمِ

In the Name of Allah, the All-Compassionate, the All-Merciful

إِذَا وَقَعَتِ ٱلۡوَاقِعَةُ ١ لَيۡسَ لِوَقۡعَتِهَا كَاذِبَةٌ ٢ خَافِضَةٞ رَّافِعَةٌ ٣

إِذَا رُجَّتِ ٱلۡأَرۡضُ رَجّٗا ٤ وَبُسَّتِ ٱلۡجِبَالُ بَسّٗا ٥ فَكَانَتۡ هَبَآءٗ

مُّنۢبَثّٗا ٦

1. (Beware of the time) When the inevitable (and the promised) Event shall come to pass.
2. There is no denying its coming to pass.
3. (This Event shall be) lowering (the status of some) and exalting (that of others).
4. (This will take place) when the Earth shall be shaken with a violent shaking,
5. And the mountains shall be completely shattered,
6. Such that they shall all be reduced to particles of dust scattered about.

Thinking Points

There is a selection of words in this section we should pay extra attention to:

1. The word *'khāfiḍa'* found in the third verse comes from *'khafadha'* which means 'to bring something down' or 'pull something down.'
2. The word *'rāfiʿah'* – also found in the third verse – comes from *'rafaʿah'* which means 'to bring something up' or 'raise something up.'
3. The word *'rajja'* which is found in the fourth verse refers to 'an intense and powerful shaking' and 'something being uprooted.'
4. The word *'bassa'* found in the fifth verse means 'crushing because of extreme pressure.'
5. The word *'habāʾa'* mentioned in the sixth verse is said to be 'soft soil-like dust or particles in the air.'
6. Lastly, the word *'manbath'* found at the end of the sixth verse means 'scattered.'

Oftentimes in the Quran, whenever an incident that will occur in the future is spoken about, the past tense verb is used. Therefore, when reading the Quran, we will find that many verses about Resurrection and the Day of Judgement are expressed in the past tense verb. Thus, in the first verse of this chapter, Allah ﷻ states: "(Beware of the time) When the inevitable (and the promised) Event shall come to pass" – and He does so using the past tense verb "come to pass" *(waqaʿat).*

The phrase: "There is no denying its coming to pass," means that when people see the events before the end of this world, they will have complete belief in it – as it is happening right in front of their eyes.

There are numerous examples in the Quran in which this style of speaking is used, meaning the past tense verb is employed. For example, in Sūrah Ghāfir, Allah ﷻ says: "So when they saw Our punishment, they said: 'We believe in Allah alone, and we reject (all) that we used to associate with Him.'"[5]

In Sūrah al-Shū'arā', Allah ﷻ states: "They will not believe in it until they see the painful punishment."[6]

In yet another verse, the Almighty says: "And those who disbelieve will continue to have doubt about it until the Hour overtakes them suddenly, or there comes to them the punishment of a destructive Day."[7]

Imam 'Alī ibn Ḥusayn al-Sajjād ؑ said: "By Allah! The Day of Resurrection will bring down the enemies of Allah into Hell [this is understood from the word *khāfiḍa*], while the friends of Allah will be elevated into the gardens of Paradise [this is understood from the word *rāfi'ah*]."[8]

Truly, dignity or disgrace – raising a person to a high ranking or degrading one to a low rank – will be made clear

---

[5] Quran, Sūrah Ghāfir (40), Verse 84:

﴿فَلَمَّا رَأَوْا بَأْسَنَا قَالُوا آمَنَّا بِاللَّهِ وَحْدَهُ وَكَفَرْنَا بِمَا كُنَّا بِهِ مُشْرِكِينَ﴾

[6] Quran, Sūrah al-Shū'arā' (26), Verse 201:

﴿لَا يُؤْمِنُونَ بِهِ حَتَّىٰ يَرَوُا الْعَذَابَ الْأَلِيمَ﴾

[7] Quran, Sūrah al-Ḥajj (22), Verse 55:

﴿وَلَا يَزَالُ الَّذِينَ كَفَرُوا فِي مِرْيَةٍ مِنْهُ حَتَّىٰ تَأْتِيَهُمُ السَّاعَةُ بَغْتَةً أَوْ يَأْتِيَهُمْ عَذَابُ يَوْمٍ عَقِيمٍ﴾

[8] Ḥuwayzī, 'Abd 'Alī ibn Jumu'ah al-'Arūsī al-, *Tafsīr Nūr al-Thaqalayn.*

on that Day, just as the great scholars have said: "Real poverty and richness – after all [of the actions] have been presented to Allah [on the Day of Judgement] – will be made clear."[9]

The Earth and the Mountains before the Resurrection

How does the Quran describe the events that will take place before the end of this world, as we enter the Resurrection and Day of Judgement?

The following are some details:

1. In normal circumstances, the earth is a place to rest and relax: "Have We not made the earth as a resting place?"[10]
2. The earth is normally a place upon which we can go about attaining our livelihood: "He it is Who made the earth subservient to you, so walk among its slopes, and eat of His provisions; but (be ever mindful that) to Him will be the Resurrection."[11]

---

[9] Āmidī, ʿAbdul Wāhid ibn Muḥammad al-, *Ghurar al-Ḥikm*:

أَلْفَقْرُ وَالْغِنَى بَعْدَ الْعَرْضِ عَلَى اللهِ.

[10] Quran, Sūrah al-Naba' (78), Verse 6:

﴿أَلَمْ نَجْعَلِ ٱلْأَرْضَ مِهَٰدًا ۝٦﴾

[11] Quran, Sūrah al-Mulk (67), Verse 15:

3. As this world begins to end, we start to transition to the Next World:
    a. On that Day, there will be no tranquility, the earth will become unsettled, and there will be unprecedented earthquakes. Allah, the Grand, says about that Day: "O humankind! Be conscious of your Lord (in reverence of Him). Indeed, the violent convulsion of the (final) Hour is a terrible thing."[12]
    b. The mountains, with all of their weight and deep roots that they have in the Earth, will be uprooted and swept away as the Quran makes note of: "And the mountains are removed and become like a mirage (as if they never existed)."[13]
    c. The mountains will violently collide with one another, as the Quran states: "And the Earth, and the mountains (on it) are removed, and are crushed with a single blow."[14]

﴿هُوَ ٱلَّذِى جَعَلَ لَكُمُ ٱلۡأَرۡضَ ذَلُولٗا فَٱمۡشُواْ فِى مَنَاكِبِهَا وَكُلُواْ مِن رِّزۡقِهِۦۖ وَإِلَيۡهِ ٱلنُّشُورُ ١٥﴾

[12] Quran, Sūrah al-Ḥajj (22), Verse 1:

﴿يَٰٓأَيُّهَا ٱلنَّاسُ ٱتَّقُواْ رَبَّكُمۡۚ إِنَّ زَلۡزَلَةَ ٱلسَّاعَةِ شَىۡءٌ عَظِيمٞ ١﴾

[13] Quran, Sūrah al-Naba' (78), Verse 20:

﴿وَسُيِّرَتِ ٱلۡجِبَالُ فَكَانَتۡ سَرَابًا ٢٠﴾

[14] Quran, Sūrah al-Ḥāqqah (69), Verse 14:

   d. The movement of the mountains will continue until they turn into pebbles and particles: “So they become dust scattered.”[15]
   e. As they are pulverized, those particles – due to the intense pressure they will be put under – will turn out to look like wool, fluffed up: “And the mountains will be like carded wool.”[16]
   f. These pebbles will be strewn just like dust dispersing in the air: “So they become dust scattered.”[17]
4. This chain of events is similar to what took place at the beginning of creation when there was nothing except smoke in existence: “Then He directed (His Knowledge, Will, Power, and Favour) to the heaven when it was smoke (like a cloud of gases) and ordered it and the Earth: “Come both of you, willingly or

---

﴿وَحُمِلَتِ ٱلْأَرْضُ وَٱلْجِبَالُ فَدُكَّتَا دَكَّةً وَٰحِدَةً ١٤﴾

[15] Quran, Sūrah al-Wāqiʿah (56), Verse 6:

﴿فَكَانَتْ هَبَآءً مُّنۢبَثًّا ٦﴾

[16] Quran, Sūrah al-Qāriʿah (101), Verse 5:

﴿وَتَكُونُ ٱلْجِبَالُ كَٱلْعِهْنِ ٱلْمَنفُوشِ ٥﴾

[17] Quran, Sūrah al-Wāqiʿah (56), Verse 6:

﴿فَكَانَتْ هَبَآءً مُّنۢبَثًّا ٦﴾

unwillingly!" They both said: "We have come willingly."[18]

Take Away Messages

1. There is no doubt that these events regarding the Resurrection will transpire, along with the fierce earthquakes that will accompany it. The phrase 'When the inevitable Event...' the word 'When' *(iḍhā)* accompanied by the past tense verb 'inevitable Event' *(Waqaʿat)* denotes something that will transpire.
2. Resurrection is an Event that has nothing that can be compared to it from this world [although there are similitudes that can sometimes be employed].
3. In the realm of propagation of truths to others, when we are warning them in regard to something extremely important, we need to ensure that we cut out all of the preliminaries and go straight to the discussion at hand. This can be understood from these verses of this chapter, as well as from other verses of the Quran, such as:

---

[18] Quran, Sūrah Fuṣṣilat (41), Verse 11:

﴿ثُمَّ ٱسْتَوَىٰٓ إِلَى ٱلسَّمَآءِ وَهِىَ دُخَانٌ فَقَالَ لَهَا وَلِلْأَرْضِ ٱئْتِيَا طَوْعًا أَوْ كَرْهًا قَالَتَآ أَتَيْنَا
طَآئِعِينَ ١١﴾

"The Sure Reality," [19] and "When the sun is folded up (and darkened)."[20]

4. Denial of the Resurrection only takes place in the life of this temporal world, especially when a person is living in ease and is in a state of spiritual heedlessness. However, as soon as the signs of Resurrection begin to appear, no one will be able to deny this definite Event.
5. As long as a person is alive, they can reform their ways and become better human beings and true believers. They should have conviction in the Resurrection now because once it begins to take place, there will be no other outcome for those who denied it other than shame and regret.
6. The Resurrection will be the collapse of thoughts, and a manifestation of the realities – the failure and fall of certain people, and the victory and ascension of others.
7. The earthquake before the Day of Judgement will be very severe.
8. Earthquakes, and the destruction of Earth and the mountains, are events that will take place prior to Resurrection Day.

---

[19] Quran, Sūrah al-Ḥāqqah (69), Verse 1:

﴿ٱلۡحَآقَّةُ ۝١﴾

[20] Quran, Sūrah al-Takwīr (81), Verse 1:

﴿إِذَا ٱلشَّمۡسُ كُوِّرَتۡ ۝١﴾

Part 2: Three Groups – Verses 7-16

وَكُنتُمْ أَزْوَاجًا ثَلَٰثَةً ﴿٧﴾ فَأَصْحَٰبُ ٱلْمَيْمَنَةِ مَآ أَصْحَٰبُ ٱلْمَيْمَنَةِ ﴿٨﴾
وَأَصْحَٰبُ ٱلْمَشْـَٔمَةِ مَآ أَصْحَٰبُ ٱلْمَشْـَٔمَةِ ﴿٩﴾ وَٱلسَّٰبِقُونَ
ٱلسَّٰبِقُونَ ﴿١٠﴾ أُو۟لَٰٓئِكَ ٱلْمُقَرَّبُونَ ﴿١١﴾ فِى جَنَّٰتِ ٱلنَّعِيمِ ﴿١٢﴾ ثُلَّةٌ مِّنَ
ٱلْأَوَّلِينَ ﴿١٣﴾ وَقَلِيلٌ مِّنَ ٱلْـَٔاخِرِينَ ﴿١٤﴾ عَلَىٰ سُرُرٍ مَّوْضُونَةٍ ﴿١٥﴾
مُّتَّكِـِٔينَ عَلَيْهَا مُتَقَٰبِلِينَ ﴿١٦﴾

7. And (at that time) you will be (sorted out into) three distinct categories,

8. (First) those who are blessed *(Aṣḥāb al-Maymana)* – how (lucky) the blessed will be!

9. And (then) those who are wretched *(Aṣḥāb al-Mash'ama)* – how (miserable) the condition of the wretched will be!

10. And (third) those who are foremost *(Al-Sābiqūn)* (in faith). They will be the foremost (in the Hereafter).

11. It is they who have (really) achieved nearness (to their Lord).

12. (They shall abide) In gardens of bliss.

13. A large party of them (will hail) from the early (believers).

14. While a few (of them will hail) from the later ones.

15. (They will be in the gardens seated) On thrones decorated (with gold and precious jewels).

16. (They will be) Reclining thereupon (sitting) face to face.

Thinking Points

Let us begin by looking at a few of the key words in this section:

1. The word *'maymana'* comes from *'yumn'* and it means 'blessings and felicity.'
2. The word *'mash'ama'* comes from *'shu'm'* and it means 'hardship.'

There are some commentators of the Quran who state that the meaning of these two words – *'maymana'* and *'mash'ama'* is 'right' and 'left' respectively. They note that on the Day of Judgement, the book of deeds of the good doers will be given to them in their right hand, while the book of deeds of the bad doers will be given to them in their left hand.

In addition, the reason why the countries of Yemen (coming from the word *yumn*) and Shām (present-day Syria) (coming from the word *shu'm*) are called as such is because standing at one spot facing the Ka'bah, Yemen is to the person's right, while Shām is to the person's left.

3. Another word used in this passage under review is *'thullah'* which refers to 'a group or community,' and when it is used alongside the verse that reads 'While a few (of them will hail) from the later ones' we understand this to mean 'a large community.'

4. The word *'surur'* is the plural of *'sarīr,'* and is used to refer to 'a bed that gives a person who lies on it joy and delight.'
5. The word *'mawḍhūna'* refers to 'something arranged' or 'to display jewelry.' In this regard, Imam Muḥammad al-Bāqir said: "The beds of those (who attain this high status) in Paradise will be interwoven with *durr* (a precious white stone similar to pearls) and rubies."²¹

Coming to the commentary of this section, we understand that amongst the creations of Allah, there is one group who are referred to as angels. They are all believers and submit entirely to Allah, as the Quran says: "...And they do as they are commanded (to do)."²² Secondly, there are the *jinn,* who are divided into two categories – some are believers, while others are disbelievers – as the Quran says: "And that some among us are those who submit, and some of us are the unjust (deviators)..."²³ Lastly, we have human beings who will ultimately be divided into three categories, as the Quran says in this *sūrah* under review: "And (at that time) you will be (sorted out into) three distinct categories."

---

²¹ ʿAllāmah Majlisī, *Biḥār al-Anwār,* Vol. 8, Pg. 218.
²² Quran, Sūrah al-Taḥrīm (66), Verse 6:

$$﴿...وَيَفْعَلُونَ مَا يُؤْمَرُونَ ۝﴾$$

²³ Quran, Sūrah al-Jinn (72), Verse 14:

$$﴿وَأَنَّا مِنَّا ٱلْمُسْلِمُونَ وَمِنَّا ٱلْقَٰسِطُونَ... ۝﴾$$

In addition, in Sūrah Fāṭir, we also see that humanity will be divided into three categories: "...And among them are those who are unjust to their souls; and among them are those who are moderate (and follow the middle course); yet there are others among them who are foremost in acts of goodness by the permission of Allah..."[24]

Thus, we see that one group is the oppressive sinners; another group is those in the middle and balanced; while the third group are those who are spiritually higher and exceptional.

In the Noble Quran, we see various expressions that have been used to denote the need to forge ahead and take a prominent position in matters of the life of this world. These include the following examples:

1. **Preceding in true faith:** "...(Those) who preceded us in faith..."[25]
2. **Foremost in charity and struggle *(jihād)*:** "Not alike among you are those who spent before the victory (of Mecca) and fought (and those who did not): they are more exalted in rank than those who spent

[24] Quran, Sūrah Fāṭir (35), Verse 32:

﴿...فَمِنْهُمْ ظَالِمٌ لِّنَفْسِهِۦ وَمِنْهُم مُّقْتَصِدٌ وَمِنْهُمْ سَابِقٌۢ بِٱلْخَيْرَٰتِ بِإِذْنِ ٱللَّهِ...﴾

[25] Quran, Sūrah al-Ḥashr (59), Verse 10:

﴿...سَبَقُونَا بِالْإِيمَانِ...﴾

and fought afterwards…"[26] In addition, we read: "…so for that let the aspirers aspire."[27]

3. **Rushing to perform good actions:** "…Therefore, hasten to (all that is) good…"[28]
4. **Hastening to the Divinely-promised blessings in Paradise:** "And (third) those who are foremost (in faith). (They are by all means) the foremost (in the Hereafter)."[29] In this regard, Imam al-Bāqir ؑ has been quoted as saying that: "The clearest meaning of this phrase are the Prophets of Allah."[30] In addition, Imam 'Alī ؑ considers those who rush towards the performance of the five daily prayers as being one of the manifestations of this phrase.

---

[26] Quran, Sūrah al-Ḥadīd (57), Verse 10:

﴿لَا يَسْتَوِى مِنْكُمْ مَنْ أَنْفَقَ مِنْ قَبْلِ الْفَتْحِ وَقَاتَلَ ۚ أُولَٰئِكَ أَعْظَمُ دَرَجَةً مِنَ الَّذِينَ أَنْفَقُوا مِنْ بَعْدُ وَقَاتَلُوا…﴾

[27] Quran, Sūrah al-Muṭaffifīn (83), Verse 26:

﴿…وَفِى ذَٰلِكَ فَلْيَتَنَافَسِ الْمُتَنَافِسُونَ﴾

[28] Quran, Sūrah al-Baqarah (2), Verse 148:

﴿…فَاسْتَبِقُوا الْخَيْرَاتِ…﴾

[29] Quran, Sūrah al-Wāqi'ah (56), Verse 10; Abū Ja'far Muḥammad al-Qummī, *Baṣā'ir al-Darajāt*, Pg. 448; Akbar Hāshemī Rafsanjānī, *Tafsīr Rāhnumā*:

﴿وَالسَّابِقُونَ السَّابِقُونَ﴾

[30] *Tafsīr Nūr al-Thaqalayn.*

We should note that the meaning of 'closeness' in the verse that reads: "It is they who have (really) achieved nearness (to their Lord)"[31] is closeness in rank, not closeness in physical place or proximity. Closeness to Allah ﷻ can never be achieved by mere claims – rather, it is something that has its own path and method that one must follow. In this regard, we see that in the Quran, the Jews and the Christians are quoted as saying: "...We are the children of Allah and His beloved..."[32] however, the Quran states in Sūrah al-Wāqiʿah that the most beloved and closest people [to Allah ﷻ] are those who take precedence in attaining the levels of human perfection, as Allah ﷻ says: "And those who are the foremost (in faith). They are the foremost (in the Hereafter. It is they who have really achieved nearness to their Lord)."[33]

In this division of the three groups in this chapter under review, it is interesting to note that the name of the *sābiqūn* has been mentioned last, and it is possible that this has been done because they are the smallest in number. However, when it comes to honouring them, they are spoken about first, and then the 'Companions of the Right' are mentioned,

---

[31] Quran, Sūrah al-Wāqiʿah (56), Verse 11:

﴿أُولَٰئِكَ الْمُقَرَّبُونَ﴾

[32] Quran, Sūrah al-Māʾidah (5), Verse 18:

﴿...نَحْنُ أَبْنَاءُ اللَّهِ وَأَحِبَّاؤُهُ...﴾

[33] Quran, Sūrah al-Wāqiʿah (56), Verses 10-11:

﴿وَالسَّابِقُونَ السَّابِقُونَ ۝١٠ أُولَٰئِكَ الْمُقَرَّبُونَ ۝١١﴾

and this is followed by all of the others – and this may be due to their lofty status above everyone else.

Take Away Messages

1. Being present on the Day of Judgement, and the method by which all people will be brought forth, is an event that is so definite to happen that it is as if it has already transpired. Thus, Allah ﷻ uses the past tense verb to describe it.
2. When it comes to the methodology of propagation and the way in which a person talks to others, one should always start by explaining things in a summary form and then go into the details.
3. The results of being fortunate or unfortunate, and the traits of bliss or misery, will continue long into the Day of Judgement – and we see this in the current passage of verses as the word used is *'aṣḥab'* which is the plural of the word *'ṣāḥib'* which means 'interconnected, adjoining, and something that is inseparable.'
4. Having true faith and hastening to do righteous deeds has value to it.
5. Those individuals who take precedence in the performance of honourable deeds while in this transient world will find that in the next life, they will be given precedence over others in achieving their rewards.
6. Those who go ahead of others in performing noble actions must be recognized in society as such.
7. Paradise will be the eternal place for righteous believers.

8. The spiritual ranks in Paradise that a person can attain are much better than any material blessings in Paradise. In this collection of verses, we see that the [truly] successful ones are first referred to as those who are close to Allah ﷻ,[34] then we are told that they will be residing in the gardens of Paradise.
9. We must never forget those righteous individuals who preceded us, and we should always take lessons from them and their noble lifestyles.
10. In order to stimulate excitement and love for Paradise, one should describe some of the specifics of Paradise. In this collection of verses, the quality and type of beds – *'mawḍūna,'* and how people will rest and relax – *'muraqaba'* has been mentioned.
11. The people of Paradise will be surrounded by one another such that they will face each other when sitting.
12. One of the points of etiquette of inviting and entertaining guests to one's house is to ensure that the host arranges somewhere for the guests to sit in such a way that they are comfortable and at ease.

---

[34] Quran, Sūrah al-Wāqiʿah (56), Verse 11:

﴿أُولَٰئِكَ الْمُقَرَّبُونَ﴾

Part 3: Some Pleasures of Paradise – Verses 17-24

يَطُوفُ عَلَيْهِمْ وِلْدَٰنٌ مُّخَلَّدُونَ ﴿١٧﴾ بِأَكْوَابٍ وَأَبَارِيقَ وَكَأْسٍ مِّن
مَّعِينٍ ﴿١٨﴾ لَّا يُصَدَّعُونَ عَنْهَا وَلَا يُنزِفُونَ ﴿١٩﴾ وَفَٰكِهَةٍ مِّمَّا
يَتَخَيَّرُونَ ﴿٢٠﴾ وَلَحْمِ طَيْرٍ مِّمَّا يَشْتَهُونَ ﴿٢١﴾ وَحُورٌ عِينٌ ﴿٢٢﴾ كَأَمْثَٰلِ
ٱللُّؤْلُوِ ٱلْمَكْنُونِ ﴿٢٣﴾ جَزَآءًۢ بِمَا كَانُوا۟ يَعْمَلُونَ ﴿٢٤﴾

17. There will circulate among them young boys made eternal,
18. Carrying goblets and (shining) beakers, and cups (full) of pure and clean drink from a flowing spring.
19. They will get no headache from it (their drinks), nor will they get intoxicated.
20. And (they will attain) such fruits as they choose,
21. And (with) flesh of birds, from whatever they desire.
22. And (there will be present) fair women *(houris)* with lovely large eyes;
23. The likeness of pearls, well-protected.
24. (Such will be) The reward for what they used to do.

Thinking Points

We begin by reviewing a few of the key words in this section:

1. The word *'akwāb'* is the plural of *'kūb,'* and refers to 'a cup without a handle' or 'a tube or spout,' and may resemble some types of cups that are used today to drink out of.
2. The word *'abārīq'* is the plural of *'abrīq,'* and refers to 'a dish that has handles and a spout' – like a pot.
3. The word *'ka'ṣ'* refers to 'a glass that is full of something to drink,' while the word *'maʿīn'* refers to 'a flowing spring.'
4. The word *'yuṣaddaʿūn'* comes from the word *'ṣudā''* which means 'a headache.'
5. The word *'yunzifūn'* comes from the word *'nazf,'* and means 'to give way to our intellect,' and its original meaning was 'to gradually empty the water from a well.'

The best phrase that can be used in regard to the Heavenly damsels in Paradise is to compare them to pearls in their shell – they are beautiful to look at and are illuminating, but at the same time, they are protected from those who should not be in their company and are far from the glances of individuals whom they are not attached to.

Take Away Messages

1. Those who will be responsible for welcoming the people into Paradise have certain unique qualities:
    a. They are always available.

b. They are young, attractive, and gracious.
c. Their kindness will be a continuous trait of theirs, not something temporary.
d. The servants will use various attractions and things as they attend to those in Paradise.
e. Their initial welcome of the people into Paradise will be with pure drinks.
f. That which the inhabitants of Paradise will drink have absolutely no impurities.
g. There will be a variety of foods offered to the people of Paradise, and the individuals themselves will decide what they want.
h. The servings will start with drinks, then fruits, followed by warm, deliciously cooked meals.
i. The drink will be a cup from a flowing spring.

2. Poultry (white meat) is better to eat than beef (red meat).
3. In terms of the types of food that we serve to others, it is important to give people what they like.
4. The women of Paradise are not only attractive, but they will also be virtuous and chaste.
5. All of the things in Paradise that a person wishes to engage in will be readily available there.
6. The pleasures of Paradise are perpetual, and this can be understood by words such as *'yatakhayyarūn'* and *'yashtahūn'* – both of which have been mentioned in the present tense verb, which denotes continuity and perpetuity.
7. In terms of the methodology of propagation and inviting others towards good actions, we should

never overlook the importance and impact of explaining the rewards of the next life.

Part 4: Barriers and Impediments – Verses 25-26

لَا يَسْمَعُونَ فِيهَا لَغْوًا وَلَا تَأْثِيمًا ﴿٢٥﴾ إِلَّا قِيلًا سَلَامًا سَلَامًا ﴿٢٦﴾

25. There they will hear no idle talk, nor any sinful speech.

26. But (all that they will hear is) good and pure words (of salutation) – 'Peace, peace.'

Thinking Points

The meaning of the word *'laghw'* is 'worthless speech;' while the meaning of the word *'ta'thīm'* is 'to attribute a sin to another person.'

It seems that the people of Paradise are individuals who, in the life of this world, led balanced and wholesome lives, and used their intellect before they did anything. We see in the *ḥadīth* that the intellect *('aql)* has been described in the following manner: "[The intellect] is that by which the All-Beneficent (Allah) is worshipped, and it is through (it) that Paradise is attained."[35]

We need to pause and think for a moment that in return for a lifetime of servitude to Allah ﷻ while in this world, our actions will be rewarded by comforts, welfare, and benefits in

[35] Shaykh Kulaynī, *Al-Kāfī*, Vol. 1, Pg. 11. The Arabic of this tradition is as follows:

مَا عُبِدَ بِهِ الرَّحْمٰنُ وَاكْتُسِبَ بِهِ الْجِنَانُ.

the Hereafter which will continue forever without ending. In such a scenario, if an individual still decides to give up the eternal pleasures in the next life for the temporal pleasures of this world, then that is the pinnacle of a lack of intelligence. It is exactly this meaning of loss that Allah ﷻ speaks about when He says in the Quran: "...Say: 'Indeed, the [true] losers are those who ruin their own souls and their families on the Day of Resurrection. Beware! Surely, that is the manifest loss!'"[36]

In one of the supplications that the believers have been encouraged to recite in the month of Rajab, it says: "Those who have looked for other than You (Allah) have actually run into a dead end (in their lives)."[37]

Moving on, we see that the people who will be given permission to enter Paradise will be given greetings of peace from multiple avenues:

1. From the other people of Paradise – as we read later in Sūrah al-Wāqiʿah: "And if one (the departed person) was from the Companions of the Right *(Aṣḥāb al-Yamīn* – the blessed people), then (it will be

---

[36] Quran, Surah al-Zumar (39), Verse 15:

﴿...قُلْ إِنَّ ٱلْخَـٰسِرِينَ ٱلَّذِينَ خَسِرُوٓا۟ أَنفُسَهُمْ وَأَهْلِيهِمْ يَوْمَ ٱلْقِيَـٰمَةِ ۗ أَلَا ذَٰلِكَ هُوَ ٱلْخُسْرَانُ ٱلْمُبِينُ ﴿١٥﴾﴾

[37] Shaykh ʿAbbās Qummī, *Mafātīḥ al-Jinān*, In the section of the recommended supplications to recite during the month of Rajab:

خَابَ الْوَافِدُونَ عَلَىٰ غَيْرِكَ.

said to them): 'Peace be upon you, (you are) from the Companions of the Right!'"[38]

2. From those who are the people of *A'rāf*: "...And on the elevated places *(A'rāf)*, there shall be people who will recognize everyone by their mark (appearance). Then they will call out to the companions of Paradise: 'Peace be upon you!' They have not (yet) entered therein, but they will be hoping (for this entry)."[39]
3. From the angels: "...And angels will enter upon them from every door (saying): 'Peace be upon you because of what you patiently endured (with virtues and guarded against sin in the world).' How excellent (and blissful) is the final abode (in the Hereafter)!"[40]
4. From Allah Himself: "'Peace:' a word from a Merciful Lord."[41]

---

[38] Quran, Sūrah al-Wāqi'ah (56), Verses 90-91:

﴿وَأَمَّآ إِن كَانَ مِنْ أَصْحَٰبِ ٱلْيَمِينِ ۝٩٠ فَسَلَٰمٌ لَّكَ مِنْ أَصْحَٰبِ ٱلْيَمِينِ ۝٩١﴾

[39] Quran, Sūrah al-A'rāf (7), Verse 46:

﴿...وَعَلَى ٱلْأَعْرَافِ رِجَالٌ يَعْرِفُونَ كُلًّۢا بِسِيمَىٰهُمْ ۚ وَنَادَوْا۟ أَصْحَٰبَ ٱلْجَنَّةِ أَن سَلَٰمٌ عَلَيْكُمْ ۚ لَمْ يَدْخُلُوهَا وَهُمْ يَطْمَعُونَ ۝٤٦﴾

[40] Quran, Sūrah al-Ra'd (13), Verses 23-24:

﴿...وَٱلْمَلَٰٓئِكَةُ يَدْخُلُونَ عَلَيْهِم مِّن كُلِّ بَابٍ ۝٢٣ سَلَٰمٌ عَلَيْكُم بِمَا صَبَرْتُمْ ۚ فَنِعْمَ عُقْبَى ٱلدَّارِ ۝٢٤﴾

[41] Quran, Sūrah Yāsīn (36), Verse 58:

In the verse of this passage of Sūrah al-Wāqiʿah, the meaning of the phrase: *'salāman salāman'* is either 'speech which is free of futility' or it is 'speech which is accompanied by amity and well-being.'

Take Away Messages

1. In Paradise, there is nothing that will cause a person any kind of mental anguish.
2. Normally in this temporal world, success is often accompanied by vain talk and sins; however, in the Hereafter, especially Paradise, this will not be the case.
3. Paradise is the abode of peace and tranquility; thus, a society in which peace and tranquility is flowing, and there is no vain talk or other kinds of wasteful speech is a paradisiacal society.

﴿سَلَٰمٌ قَوْلًا مِّن رَّبٍّ رَّحِيمٍ ۝٥٨﴾

Part 5: Those in Bliss – Verses 27-40

وَأَصْحَٰبُ ٱلْيَمِينِ مَآ أَصْحَٰبُ ٱلْيَمِينِ ﴿٢٧﴾ فِى سِدْرٍ مَّخْضُودٍ ﴿٢٨﴾
وَطَلْحٍ مَّنضُودٍ ﴿٢٩﴾ وَظِلٍّ مَّمْدُودٍ ﴿٣٠﴾ وَمَآءٍ مَّسْكُوبٍ ﴿٣١﴾ وَفَٰكِهَةٍ
كَثِيرَةٍ ﴿٣٢﴾ لَّا مَقْطُوعَةٍ وَلَا مَمْنُوعَةٍ ﴿٣٣﴾ وَفُرُشٍ مَّرْفُوعَةٍ ﴿٣٤﴾ إِنَّآ
أَنشَأْنَٰهُنَّ إِنشَآءً ﴿٣٥﴾ فَجَعَلْنَٰهُنَّ أَبْكَارًا ﴿٣٦﴾ عُرُبًا أَتْرَابًا ﴿٣٧﴾
لِّأَصْحَٰبِ ٱلْيَمِينِ ﴿٣٨﴾ ثُلَّةٌ مِّنَ ٱلْأَوَّلِينَ ﴿٣٩﴾ وَثُلَّةٌ مِّنَ ٱلْءَاخِرِينَ ﴿٤٠﴾

27. And the Companions of the Right – what are the Companions of the Right?

28. (They shall abide) Amidst (the land of) the thornless *Sidra* (Lote tree, a symbol of bliss).

29. And (in the garden of) layered bananas.

30. And (in) extended shades.

31. And (near) water pouring down (falling from heights).

32. And (amidst) abundant fruit.

33. (The season) which are not limited, and (they are) not forbidden.

34. And (upon) couches raised high.

35. Verily, We have made them (the women who will be for them in Paradise) excellent and have raised them into a (special new) creation.
36. And have made them virgins (pure and undefiled).
37. Devoted (to their husbands), and of equal age (matching them in every respect).
38. For the companions of the right,
39. (This group will consist of) a large party from the earlier people (of Islam).
40. And a large party from the later ones.

Thinking Points

Some of the key words in this passage that we need to understand include:

1. The meaning of the word *'sidr'* is 'a tree that casts a vast shadow.'
2. The meaning of *'makhḍūd'* is 'a plant whose leaves are broken and thorny.'
3. The meaning of *'manḍhūd'* is 'something dense.'
4. The meaning of *'maskūb'* is 'something that flows downwards like a waterfall.'
5. The meaning of *'atrāb'* is 'something similar and of the same age.'
6. The meaning of the word *'tarā'ib'* is 'the ribs in a person's rib cage' – with all of the ribs looking identical to one another.

7. The word *'ṭalḥ'* whose plural is *'ṭilḥa'* refers to 'a banana tree.' However, it should be noted that some commentators of the Quran have stated that the meaning of the word *'ṭilḥ'* refers to a tree known as *'Umm al-Ghīlān'* which is a part of the acacia family of trees – a tree or bush that has beautiful smelling flowers.[42]
8. Although the word *'furush'* is the plural of *'firāsh'* it is used in the meanings of 'the ground, an animal that one rides upon, a carpet, and a bed;' and the word *'marfū'ah'* means 'something exquisite and expensive;' however, when using these words, the Prophet ﷺ said that: "In Paradise, there are couches made of silk of various colours which will be placed across from one another."[43] With that said, in this verse the apparent meaning of *'furush'* is 'one's spouse;' while the meaning of *'marfū'ah'* is 'the value and worth of that individual due to their intellect, perfection, and beauty,' and this is better understood from the verse that follows: "Verily, We have made them (the spouses in Paradise) excellent and have raised them into a (special new) creation."[44]

---

[42] *Tafsīr Rāhnumā.*

[43] *Tafsīr Nūr al-Thaqalayn*; *Al-Kāfī*, Vol. 2, Pg. 97.

[44] Quran, Sūrah al-Wāqi'ah (56), Verse 35:

﴿إِنَّا أَنْشَأْنَاهُنَّ إِنْشَاءً﴾

9. The word *"ʿurub'* whose plural is *"ʿurūb'* refers to 'a woman who is smiling, jovial, and intensely in love with her husband, and is unpretentious with him.'

Those who are the Companions of the Right *(Aṣḥāb al-Yamīn)* are the same people spoken about in verse 8 and referred to as *Aṣḥāb al-Maymanah.* Since on the Day of Resurrection, the book of deeds of the righteous doers will be given to them in their right hand and they will be considered as the people of blessings and happiness, for this reason they are called the *Aṣḥāb al-Yamīn* – which literally means 'Companions of the Right.'

When it comes to the inhabitants of Paradise, a question may arise as to what age will people be there? There is an understanding in Islam that there will be no old people in Paradise, and in this regard, there is a *ḥadīth* where the Prophet ﷺ said to his wife, Umm Salama: "On the Day of Judgement, Allah will transform the old, grey haired believing women into young, beautiful ladies."[45]

To conclude the discussion about the rewards promised to the ones in proximity to Allah ﷻ *(al-Muqarrabūn),* it was mentioned: "(Such will be) the reward for what they used to do."[46]

Thus, all of the rewards and blessings that they will receive in the Hereafter are due to their own actions that they performed while in this world.

---

[45] *Tafsīr Nūr al-Thaqalayn.*

[46] Quran, Sūrah al-Wāqiʿah (56), Verse 24:

﴿جَزَاءً بِمَا كَانُوا يَعْمَلُونَ﴾

However, it must be noted that at the conclusion of these verses that we are currently reviewing, after speaking about all of the blessings that have been promised to the Companions of the Right, we do not see the phrase: 'a reward because of your actions...' – thus, it can be said that the blessings of this group under discussion are actually a Divine grace from the Almighty to them.

One thing we should keep in mind is that worldly blessings are often accompanied by some sort of hindrances; however, in Paradise, the blessings have no flaws or obstacles in them whatsoever. For example:

1. In this world, some plants and rose bushes have thorns – however, the plants in Paradise will not have these.
2. In this world, when we find shade, it is not permanent – however, in Paradise, the shade of the trees will be perpetual.
3. In this world, fruits are either seasonal or hard to find in certain places – however, in the afterlife, the fruits will be plentiful and perpetual, and easy to get without any exertion.
4. Oftentimes, a person's spouse in this world is not necessarily compatible with them – however, in Paradise, spouses will be fully compatible with each other in all ways – as they are referred to as *'atrāb'* or 'equal.' Sometimes, love for one's spouse is just not there – but in Paradise, couples will truly love one another – and this is referred to in this passage as *'ūrub'* which means 'devoted.'

Since the Prophets sent by Allah ﷻ were numerous in number (124,000), we know that their successors *(awṣiyā')* were also large in number. Thus, when speaking about the quantity of the *Muqarrabīn*, Allah ﷻ says: "A large party of them (will hail) from the early (believers), while a few (of them will hail) from the later ones."

Thus, those who are the *Muqarrabīn* will be more from the previous generations compared to those from the community of the Muslims.

Take Away Messages

1. In the Hereafter, those who are the 'Companions of the Right' *(Aṣḥāb al-Yamīn)* will have a lofty, wonderful position.
2. Although scholars have delved into some of the benefits that can be derived from the leaves of a Lote tree, more research needs to be done to better understand what effects this tree has on air quality, and on the environment in general.
3. Flowing water is much cleaner and purer than stagnant, standing water.
4. Paradise and its blessings have been created by Allah ﷻ from time immemorial and are ready to be enjoyed by the people who make it there.
5. The chastity that spouses in Paradise have will be continuous, and will always remain with them - otherwise what difference would this make from the spouses that we have in this transient world?
6. The world is never devoid of righteous individuals.

Part 6: The Wretched People – Verses 41-48

وَأَصۡحَٰبُ ٱلشِّمَالِ مَآ أَصۡحَٰبُ ٱلشِّمَالِ ﴿٤١﴾ فِي سَمُومٖ وَحَمِيمٖ ﴿٤٢﴾
وَظِلّٖ مِّن يَحۡمُومٖ ﴿٤٣﴾ لَّا بَارِدٖ وَلَا كَرِيمٍ ﴿٤٤﴾ إِنَّهُمۡ كَانُواْ قَبۡلَ ذَٰلِكَ
مُتۡرَفِينَ ﴿٤٥﴾ وَكَانُواْ يُصِرُّونَ عَلَى ٱلۡحِنثِ ٱلۡعَظِيمِ ﴿٤٦﴾ وَكَانُواْ يَقُولُونَ
أَئِذَا مِتۡنَا وَكُنَّا تُرَابٗا وَعِظَٰمًا أَءِنَّا لَمَبۡعُوثُونَ ﴿٤٧﴾ أَوَ ءَابَآؤُنَا
ٱلۡأَوَّلُونَ ﴿٤٨﴾

41. But as for the Companions of the Left – what are the Companions of the Left?

42. (They shall dwell) In (painfully) scorching fire and scalding water.

43. And (under) the shadow of black smoke,

44. (Which is) Neither cool (to refresh), nor pleasant.

45. Indeed, they lived a life of ease and abundance before this (in the present world),

46. And (they) used to persist in extreme sinfulness.

47. And they used to say: ‘When we die and are reduced to dust and bones, shall we then be raised to life (again)?

48. And our forefathers (as well will be raised to a new life with us)?'

Thinking Points

Let us first review some key words in this passage:

1. The word *'samūm'* refers to 'a burning wind' that, just like poison that enters the body, completely pierces through the person, while the Arabic word *'masām'* refers to 'the pores in one's body' (and comes from the same root as the word *samūm*).
2. The word *'ḥamīm'* refers to 'boiling, extremely hot water.'
3. The word *'yaḥmūm'* is 'thick, black smoke.'
4. The word *'mutraf'* refers to 'a person who has been given innumerable blessings – however, they still fall into a state of spiritual heedlessness.'
5. The word *'ḥinth'* refers to 'a major sin' – and most often, it is used regarding breaking one's oath and going against one's pledge.
6. The word *'yuṣirrūn'* comes from the root *'iṣrār,'* and this word has been used four times in the Quran for 'the continuance of performance of sins.'

On the Day of Judgement, the wretched ones (also known as *Aṣḥāb al-Shimāl* – Companions of the Left) will experience extreme punishments and chastisements such as burning fire, boiling water, and thick, dark, sweltering smoke.[47]

---

[47] Marāghī, Aḥmad Muṣṭafā al-, *Tafsīr Marāghī.*

As mentioned previously, the style of the Quran is such that when it speaks about future events and occurrences, it talks about them as having happened in the past. Even the Day of Judgement is explained in such a way as if the guilty people are already present and have had their files adjudicated, their records of deeds have been closed and sealed, and their sentences have been passed down – and it is as if they are already engulfed in the painful punishments.

Comparison between the People of Heaven and Hell

At this point, by turning our attention to various verses of the Quran, let us put forth a comparison between the people referred to as *Aṣḥāb al-Yamīn* who will be in Paradise, and *Aṣḥāb al-Shimāl* who will be in Hell:

Companions of the Right - The Righteous Ones - Aṣḥāb al-Yamīn	Companions of the Left - The Iniquitous Ones - Aṣḥāb al-Shimāl
Living in elongated and perpetual, cool, shade[48]	Surrounded by shade from thick, dark smoke[49]

[48] Quran, Sūrah al-Wāqiʿah (56), Verse 30:

﴿وَظِلٍّ مَّمْدُودٍ ۝٣٠﴾

"And in extended shades."

[49] Quran, Sūrah al-Wāqiʿah (56), Verse 43:

﴿وَظِلٍّ مِّن يَحْمُومٍ ۝٤٣﴾

"And (under) the shadow of black smoke."

Provided with a continuous supply of fruits[50]	No comforts – neither cooling, nor of any benefit[51]
A steady flow of pure drinks[52]	Boiling, molten metal to drink[53]

[50] Quran, Sūrah al-Wāqiʿah (56), Verse 33:

﴿لَّا مَقْطُوعَةٍ وَلَا مَمْنُوعَةٍ﴾

"Never cut off, nor forbidden."

[51] Quran, Sūrah al-Wāqiʿah (56), Verse 44:

﴿لَّا بَارِدٍ وَلَا كَرِيمٍ﴾

"(A shadow) which is neither cool (to refresh), nor pleasant."

[52] Quran, Sūrah al-Insān (76), Verse 21:

﴿...وَسَقَىٰهُمْ رَبُّهُمْ شَرَابًا طَهُورًا﴾

"...and their Lord will favour them with a purifying drink."

[53] Quran, Sūrah al-Kahf (18), Verse 29:

﴿...وَإِن يَسْتَغِيثُوا۟ يُغَاثُوا۟ بِمَآءٍ كَٱلْمُهْلِ يَشْوِى ٱلْوُجُوهَ ۚ بِئْسَ ٱلشَّرَابُ وَسَآءَتْ مُرْتَفَقًا﴾

"...If they beg for water, they will be given water like molten metal that scalds their faces. How dreadful a drink, and how evil is the resting place."

Streams of pure, clean, water[54]	People begging for water[55]
Rivers of milk[56]	Endless supply of putrid, boiling water[57]
Rivers of pure wine[58]	Drinks made from pus and blood[59]

---

[54] Quran, Sūrah Muḥammad (47), Verse 15:

﴿مَّثَلُ ٱلْجَنَّةِ ٱلَّتِى وُعِدَ ٱلْمُتَّقُونَ ۖ فِيهَآ أَنْهَٰرٌ مِّن مَّآءٍ غَيْرِ ءَاسِنٍ وَأَنْهَٰرٌ مِّن لَّبَنٍ لَّمْ يَتَغَيَّرْ
طَعْمُهُۥ وَأَنْهَٰرٌ مِّنْ خَمْرٍ لَّذَّةٍ لِّلشَّٰرِبِينَ وَأَنْهَٰرٌ مِّنْ عَسَلٍ مُّصَفًّى...﴿١٥﴾﴾

"A likeness of Paradise which the righteous are promised, wherein are rivers of water imperishable (in taste, colour, and smell); and rivers of milk whose taste never changes; and rivers of wine delicious for the drinkers; and rivers of pure, clear honey..."

[55] Quran, Sūrah al-A'rāf (7), Verse 50:

﴿وَنَادَىٰٓ أَصْحَٰبُ ٱلنَّارِ أَصْحَٰبَ ٱلْجَنَّةِ أَنْ أَفِيضُوا۟ عَلَيْنَا مِنَ ٱلْمَآءِ أَوْ مِمَّا رَزَقَكُمُ
ٱللَّهُ... ﴿٥٠﴾﴾

"And the Companions of the Fire call out to the Companions of Paradise: 'Pour upon us some water, or something from whatever Allah has provided for you...'"

[56] Quran, Sūrah Muḥammad (47), Verse 15 (See above).

[57] Quran, Sūrah Ṣuād (38), Verse 57:

﴿هَٰذَا فَلْيَذُوقُوهُ حَمِيمٌ وَغَسَّاقٌ﴿٥٧﴾﴾

"This (then is for them), so let them taste it – boiling water and intensely cold, dark fluid."

[58] Quran, Sūrah Muḥammad (47), Verse 15 (See above).

[59] Quran, Sūrah al-Ḥāqqah (69), Verse 36:

Rivers of pure honey[60]	Vile water (containing pus)[61]
Two vast, lush gardens[62]	A constricted place[63]
Nothing but peace, peace[64]	They will curse others for their miserable state[65]

﴿وَلَا طَعَامٌ إِلَّا مِنْ غِسْلِينٍ ۝٣٦﴾

"Nor any food except foul pus."

[60] Quran, Sūrah Muḥammad (47), Verse 15 (See previous page).

[61] Quran, Sūrah Ibrāhīm (14), Verse 16:

﴿مِّن وَرَآئِهِۦ جَهَنَّمُ وَيُسْقَىٰ مِن مَّآءٍ صَدِيدٍ ۝١٦﴾

"And Hell is awaiting them, and they will be made to drink of oozing pus,"

[62] Quran, Sūrah al-Raḥmān (55), Verse 62:

﴿وَمِن دُونِهِمَا جَنَّتَانِ ۝٦٢﴾

"And besides these two, there are yet two (other) gardens."

[63] Quran, Sūrah al-Furqān (25), Verse 13:

﴿وَإِذَآ أُلْقُوا۟ مِنْهَا مَكَانًا ضَيِّقًا مُّقَرَّنِينَ دَعَوْا۟ هُنَالِكَ ثُبُورًا ۝١٣﴾

"And when they are flung, chained together, into a narrow place in it, they will pray there for destruction (extinction)."

[64] Quran, Sūrah al-Wāqiʿah (56), Verse 26:

﴿إِلَّا قِيلًا سَلَٰمًا سَلَٰمًا ۝٢٦﴾

"But (all that they will hear is) good and pure words (of salutation) - 'Peace, peace.'"

[65] Quran, Sūrah al-Aʿrāf (7), Verse 38:

Entrance with respect[66]	Entrance being shown wrath and vengeance[67]
A meeting with mercy and Divine greetings from the Lord[68]	Despised and not given permission to speak to the Lord[69]

﴿...كُلَّمَا دَخَلَتْ أُمَّةٌ لَّعَنَتْ أُخْتَهَا...﴿٣٨﴾﴾

"...Every time a community enters the Fire, it curses its fellow community (who went before it) ..."

[66] Quran, Sūrah al-Zumar (39), Verse 73:

﴿...حَتَّىٰٓ إِذَا جَآءُوهَا وَفُتِحَتْ أَبْوَٰبُهَا وَقَالَ لَهُمْ خَزَنَتُهَا سَلَٰمٌ عَلَيْكُمْ طِبْتُمْ فَٱدْخُلُوهَا خَٰلِدِينَ﴿٧٣﴾﴾

"...Until when they arrive there, its doors will be opened (as sheer grace from Allah), and its keepers will welcome them saying: 'Peace be upon you, you have become pure, so enter it (Paradise) to abide therein eternally!'"

[67] Quran, Sūrah al-Ḥāqqah (69), Verse 30:

﴿خُذُوهُ فَغُلُّوهُ﴿٣٠﴾﴾

"(And the command will come): 'Lay hold of him and shackle him!'"

[68] Quran, Sūrah Yāsīn (36), Verse 58:

﴿سَلَٰمٌ قَوْلًا مِّن رَّبٍّ رَّحِيمٍ﴿٥٨﴾﴾

"'Peace,' a word from an All-Merciful Lord."

[69] Quran, Sūrah al-Mu'minūn (23), Verse 108:

﴿قَالَ ٱخْسَـُٔوا۟ فِيهَا وَلَا تُكَلِّمُونِ﴿١٠٨﴾﴾

Unparalleled welcoming and embracing by the servants[70]	Going around areas of fire and burning water[71]

Take Away Messages

1. On the Day of Judgement, a group of people will be humiliated, and their book of deeds will be given to them in their left hand due to their own destructive actions in this world.
2. The state of those going to Hell will be so frightful that it will be a point of astonishment for other people.
3. The punishments after the accounting on the Day of Judgement will be extremely difficult to bear, and this can be understood by the two words that have been used: *'samūm'* and *'ḥamīm,'* as they are mentioned in the indefinite form of the noun which shows the intensity and seriousness of the punishment.

"He will say: 'Remain despised therein and do not speak to Me.'"

[70] Quran, Sūrah al-Insān (76), Verse 19:

﴿وَيَطُوفُ عَلَيْهِمْ وِلْدَانٌ مُّخَلَّدُونَ إِذَا رَأَيْتَهُمْ حَسِبْتَهُمْ لُؤْلُؤًا مَّنثُورًا ١٩﴾

"There will go around them youths of perpetual freshness; when you see them, you would think them (to be as beautiful as) scattered pearls."

[71] Quran, Sūrah al-Raḥmān (55), Verse 44:

﴿يَطُوفُونَ بَيْنَهَا وَبَيْنَ حَمِيمٍ ءَانٍ ٤٤﴾

"They will go around it (the fire), and hot, boiling water."

4. The carefree, spiritually-intoxicated individuals must realize that their spiritual heedlessness and apparent success in the life of this world will only cause them humiliation and suffering in the world to come.
5. What makes sins weightier and even more dangerous for an individual are the continuous performance of those evil actions.
6. Allah ﷻ is All-Just, and the punishments that a person will face are because of their own actions. Those who act against the Divine ordinances will be inflicted with three types of punishments: burning winds or fire, boiling waters, and scorching shade; and these are all because they performed impermissible actions in their lives while in this transient world.
7. Well-being and prosperity will be removed from a person in this world through the performance of sins and doubting the Resurrection and Day of Judgement.
8. Those who deny the Day of Accountability have no proof to do so and only assume it to be something that is not possible.
9. If a person were to disbelieve and keep it to themselves, then it is 'harmless.' However, the real danger lies when such an individual begins to promote such thoughts within society and becomes the reason for others to deviate as well.
10. Those who are skeptical about religion often expand the scope of doubt to others as well.

Part 7: Everyone will be Brought Back – Verses 49-50

قُلْ إِنَّ ٱلْأَوَّلِينَ وَٱلْآخِرِينَ ﴿٤٩﴾ لَمَجْمُوعُونَ إِلَىٰ مِيقَٰتِ يَوْمٍ مَّعْلُومٍ ﴿٥٠﴾

49. Say: 'Most surely, the earlier people and the later ones,

50. Shall all be gathered together at the fixed time of an appointed Day.'

Thinking Points

The Noble Quran then instructs the Prophet of Islam ﷺ to respond to those who reject His Message and say to them that it is not only them, but also their forefathers, as well as the former and later generations who will all be resurrected.

The term *'miqāt'* comes from the Arabic root word for 'time' *(waqt)* and refers to a specific time set for an action or promise. Here, it indicates the 'appointed time of the Day of Judgement' when everyone will gather in the assembly for the reckoning of their deeds. Sometimes, this word is used metaphorically to refer to places designated for specific purposes, such as the *miqāt* for *Ḥajj*, which are four specific locations where pilgrims enter into the state of *iḥrām.*

Additionally, from the emphatic expressions that Allah ﷻ uses in this verse, such as the particle *'innā'* after the imperative verb of 'Say' *(qul),* and the *'lām'* which comes at the start of the word 'All be gathered together' *(lamajmuʿūn)*, we are given multiple confirmations about the reality of the Day of Judgement.

It is evident from this verse that the resurrection of all of humanity will occur simultaneously on a single day. This same concept appears in other verses of the Quran as well, and it is clear that those who assume that the resurrection will happen at separate times for each nation are unfamiliar with the teachings of the Quran. For example, we see the following verses in the Book of Allah ﷻ: "That is how your Lord seizes the townships when He seizes them while they are wrongdoers. His seizing is indeed painful, severe."[72]

In addition: "And every one of them will appear before Him on the Day of Judgement all alone."[73]

It almost goes without saying that the knowledge of the Resurrection and Day of Judgement belongs only to Allah ﷻ, and no one – not even the Prophets, Imams, or the closest angels – know its exact time.

Take Away Messages

1. Even if doubts that stem from stubbornness are brought up by other people, we must ensure that we

---

[72] Quran, Sūrah Hūd (11), Verse 102:

﴿وَكَذَٰلِكَ أَخْذُ رَبِّكَ إِذَآ أَخَذَ ٱلْقُرَىٰ وَهِىَ ظَٰلِمَةٌ ۚ إِنَّ أَخْذَهُۥٓ أَلِيمٌ شَدِيدٌ ﴿١٠٢﴾﴾

[73] Quran, Sūrah Maryam (19), Verse 95:

﴿وَكُلُّهُمْ ءَاتِيهِ يَوْمَ ٱلْقِيَٰمَةِ فَرْدًا ﴿٩٥﴾﴾

offer a definitive answer to them and do not allow such thoughts to linger without a response.

2. The Power of Allah ﷻ is such that for Him, bringing back to life those from the early generations or the later ones is one in the same.
3. All of humanity – from the beginning of time to the end – will be gathered together on a specific day.
4. Although the exact time for when the Day of Judgement will take place is not known to anyone, it is something that is clear, defined, and known to Allah ﷻ.

Part 8: An Unbearable Punishment – Verses 51-56

ثُمَّ إِنَّكُمْ أَيُّهَا ٱلضَّآلُّونَ ٱلْمُكَذِّبُونَ ﴿٥١﴾ لَأَكِلُونَ مِن شَجَرٍ مِّن
زَقُّومٍ ﴿٥٢﴾ فَمَالِـُٔونَ مِنْهَا ٱلْبُطُونَ ﴿٥٣﴾ فَشَٰرِبُونَ عَلَيْهِ مِنَ ٱلْحَمِيمِ ﴿٥٤﴾
فَشَٰرِبُونَ شُرْبَ ٱلْهِيمِ ﴿٥٥﴾ هَٰذَا نُزُلُهُمْ يَوْمَ ٱلدِّينِ ﴿٥٦﴾

51. Then indeed you, O those (gone) astray (who are) deniers (of the truth).
52. You will certainly eat from the trees of *zaqqūm*,
53. And will fill your bellies with it.
54. Then you shall drink over it, the boiling water,
55. And will drink like the drinking of thirsty camels (who are suffering from insatiable thirst).
56. This will be their (the wretched ones') entertainment on the Day of Requital.

Thinking Points

There are a few words in this section that we need to review to better understand this portion of the chapter:

1. The term *'zaqqūm'* is a reference to 'a bitter, putrid, and bad-tasting plant' that will cause the body of a person to become inflamed if merely its juice touches

one. This plant is considered to be the food of those who will go to Hell.

2. The word *'nuzul'* is used to refer to 'those things that are prepared as a way to welcome guests.'
3. The word *'hīm'* is the 'name of a sickness that camels are afflicted with' in which, no matter how much water they drink, they never become satiated, and they end up dying in this state. This word is also used in regard to porous ground which is covered in sand or pebbles, and no matter how much water you pour onto it, it continues to seep into the ground.

In this passage of the Quran, it is made clear that the bitter and horrible foods of this world that people do not like to eat or cannot eat – and things much worse than them – will be fed to sinners in the Hereafter.

4. The letter *'lām'* at the beginning of the phrase *'la ākilūn'* means that a person will want to eat less – however, in the next life, an individual will be made to eat to one's fill (from this tree) – and they will continuously have to eat from this tree, even though they may want to stop.
5. The verse which reads: "And fill your stomach with it," means that even though they will want to eat other foods in its place, the only other item that will be served to them is boiling water.
6. The phrase of the verse which reads "the boiling water" (*min al-ḥamīm)* tells us what kind of drink these people will be given. What is more than that is these people will continuously drink to their heart's content but will be so thirsty just like a thirsty camel

arriving at a watering well that they will drink all of the burning water up and still not be satiated.

7. Lastly, the phrase *'shurb al-hīm'* means 'just like a camel with the sickness of not being quenched of its intense thirst.' This is exactly how these people will react to the food from *al-zaqqūm* – not only will that be their food, but they will have to 'quench' their thirst with boiling water.

Take Away Messages

1. The people in Hell will be addressed with the toughest and most humiliating forms of words when spoken to by Allah ﷻ, or angels.
2. The wretched people – also known as Companions of the Left – are misguided. Multiple times – every single day – Muslims ask Allah ﷻ for the ability to not be among those who are the misguided ones, as we see in Sūrah al-Fātiḥa (Chapter 1), Verse 7.
3. Even worse than being misguided is to deny the truth, and if this was not the case, then many of those who are misguided would have had the blessings of being guided.
4. If all of the mental humiliations and physical retributions are merely preliminaries in order to welcome the wretched people (Companions of the Left), then one can only imagine the welcome they will be given when they are actually taken into Hell.
5. Allah ﷻ is All-Just *('Ādil)*, and the punishments that He metes out are also based on His Justice. Thus, all

of the difficulties that a person faces are really the outcome of one's own actions, and that Day will be the ultimate Day of rewards and retributions.

Part 9: The Proofs – Verses 57-60

نَحْنُ خَلَقْنَٰكُمْ فَلَوْلَا تُصَدِّقُونَ ۝٥٧ أَفَرَءَيْتُم مَّا تُمْنُونَ ۝٥٨ ءَأَنتُمْ
تَخْلُقُونَهُۥٓ أَمْ نَحْنُ ٱلْخَٰلِقُونَ ۝٥٩ نَحْنُ قَدَّرْنَا بَيْنَكُمُ ٱلْمَوْتَ وَمَا
نَحْنُ بِمَسْبُوقِينَ ۝٦٠

57. We created you (the first time), so why do you not then realize the reality (of the Resurrection).

58. Have you seen (given thought) to what (the sperm) you emit?

59. Is it you who creates it, or are We the Creator (of it)?

60. We have ordained death for you (all); and We cannot be stopped from (that).

Thinking Points

It was explained in the previous verses that the wretched people, Companions of the Left, had doubts regarding the Resurrection, and they used to say: "When we die and our bodies have decayed and turned into dust, is it realistic to believe that we will be brought back to life again!?"

Thus, from verse 57 of this chapter and beyond, Allah ﷻ presents numerous examples of His Power in this temporal world so as to remove any doubts people may have about the Resurrection and the Day of Judgement taking place.

The proofs that the Quran presents transcend time and place – they are neither limited to a particular era, nor are they only for a specific geographic location. Whether it be a fetus in the womb, or a germinated seed in the ground, the Quranic proofs are relevant to all times and places and are simple and clear for everyone to understand.

As for the portion under review, this section of verses looks at two junctures of our lives: our end and our beginning.

Although the verses address the creation of life, since they are intertwined with the concept of death and resurrection, we will look at this first, then move on to our creation, through the natural process that Allah ﷻ has put in place for humanity to reproduce:

1. **As it relates to death:** Some people have questioned why, despite the fact that we know lots of facts, are we deprived from knowing exactly when we will die? In response to this important question, we state that there is wisdom behind why the actual time of our death has been kept hidden from all of us, and there are many benefits to this. From one point of view, it makes an individual be prepared that at any time, death may approach them. However, it also allows a person to have a normal daily life schedule because one will not be waiting for a certain time to die. Imagine what a bitter experience life would be if one knew the exact instance when they will leave this world.
2. **When it comes to life:** Although some of the preliminaries that are required to create the next

generation of people, such as the act of sexual intercourse and the fertilization of an egg by the sperm in the womb of a woman, is done directly by the human being, the inoculation of the sperm and the egg, and its growth in several stages, and its maintenance and growth into a perfectly formed human being with its unique characteristics are all the work of Allah ﷻ.

Let it be noted that even if a human being was to grow outside of the womb, this would still not diminish the Power of Allah ﷻ in the least and does not bring to question His Authority over creation. This is all in the control of Allah ﷻ because a human being does not play any role in the designing stages of creation – they play a role in the natural act of procreation; however, it is Allah ﷻ who has permitted them to do so, and ultimately, He is the real Creator.

Take Away Messages

1. Why do people have doubts regarding the Resurrection? The One who created everyone in the first instance can easily bring them back into creation once again.
2. We must speak to the deniers and those who do not believe, and we must present to them solid and concrete proof.
3. The act of reprimanding should always come after providing the necessary evidence – in this passage we first see that Allah ﷻ says: "(It is) We who created you

(the first time)," then He says: "Why do you not then realize the reality (of the Resurrection)."

4. When it comes to providing proof, one should never suffice with only one proof or one example.
5. When it comes to propagation of the teachings of religion and respectful disputation with other people, we should make use of various literary tools such as asking questions, so as to awaken and call upon the conscience of individuals.
6. The Power of Allah ﷻ can be seen in the act of creation and in the taking of lives.
7. Death is an event that is not by chance – it is carried out with wisdom, is calculated, and has been pre-ordained.
8. The end of a person's life and the time of death are **only** in the Hands of Allah ﷻ.
9. The death of a human being does not signal the inability of Allah ﷻ to keep the person alive, rather it is a wisdom-filled, pre-determined reality.
10. The Power of Allah ﷻ is absolute, and there is no individual who can flee death; and in this, the determination of Allah ﷻ takes precedence and surpasses everyone and everything else.

Part 10: Being Brought Back – Verses 61-62

عَلَىٰٓ أَن نُّبَدِّلَ أَمْثَٰلَكُمْ وَنُنشِئَكُمْ فِى مَا لَا تَعْلَمُونَ ﴿٦١﴾ وَلَقَدْ
عَلِمْتُمُ ٱلنَّشْأَةَ ٱلْأُولَىٰ فَلَوْلَا تَذَكَّرُونَ ﴿٦٢﴾

61. From replacing you with beings similar to you, (or from) evolving you into a form which is unknown to you (at present).

62. And you certainly know about the first creation. Then, why do you not reflect?

Thinking Points

There is an interpretation of verse 61 that commentators of the Quran have offered that states that it is a continuation of the previous verse which reads: "We have ordained death for you (all); and We cannot be stopped from (that)."

Other commentators of the Quran note that verse 61 is independent and has been used by Allah ﷻ to outline the purpose of what was mentioned in the previous verse. Based on this interpretation, we could understand verse 61 of this chapter as saying: "We are never incapable or overpowered to replace one group of people with another to take the place of the previous generation."

Regarding the phrase: "...Replacing you with beings similar to you..." there are two interpretations that commentators of the Quran have provided:

1. The commonly accepted interpretation is that it refers to replacing people in this world – such that people habituated to evil will be replaced with people of goodness.
2. The second interpretation states that "similar others" refers to human beings themselves, who will return in the afterlife. The term "similar" is used because human beings will not return exactly as they were, but rather in a different time with new physical and spiritual makeup.

However, the first interpretation seems more fitting.

In any case, the goal of this section is to present an argument for the Day of Resurrection through the phenomenon of death. The argument can be explained as follows: The Wise God, Allah ﷻ, who created humanity, and continuously replaces one generation with another through death, must have a purpose behind what He does. If this purpose were limited to merely this worldly life, then it would make sense for human life to be eternal rather than living for such a brief amount of time, mixed with countless hardships. Such an existence would hardly justify this cycle of comings and goings of generations after generations. Thus, the law of death strongly indicates that this world is a passage, not a destination; a bridge, not an endpoint; for if it were the final destination, then it would have been everlasting.

The phrase "...evolve you into a form which is not known to you..." may refer to the creation of human beings in the Hereafter, which could serve as a purpose for the life and death of this world.

Obviously, since no one has seen the Hereafter, we remain unaware of the principles and systems governing it, and as such, its true nature cannot even be fully conveyed through our words – we can only glimpse a shadow of it from afar.

Additionally, this verse clearly illustrates the reality that you will be created in a new world – with forms and conditions unknown to you.

Take Away Messages

1. The philosophy of death is the replacement of one group of people and the emergence of a new generation.
2. The Power of Allah ﷻ in being able to replace death with life is also proof for the Power of Allah ﷻ in bringing about the resurrection.
3. The life of this world is simply a place of passage filled with trials and tests – not a stopping ground, nor our final destination.

Part 11: Ever Thought About… – Verses 63-67

أَفَرَءَيْتُم مَّا تَحْرُثُونَ ﴿٦٣﴾ ءَأَنتُمْ تَزْرَعُونَهُۥٓ أَمْ نَحْنُ ٱلزَّٰرِعُونَ ﴿٦٤﴾ لَوْ
نَشَآءُ لَجَعَلْنَٰهُ حُطَٰمًا فَظَلْتُمْ تَفَكَّهُونَ ﴿٦٥﴾ إِنَّا لَمُغْرَمُونَ ﴿٦٦﴾ بَلْ
نَحْنُ مَحْرُومُونَ ﴿٦٧﴾

63. Have you ever given thought to that which you plant (in the ground)?

64. Is it you who cause it to grow or is it We who are the Growers?

65. If We (so) willed We could make it (dry) debris (before it is ripe and ready to be harvested); then you would remain wondering.

66. (Saying): 'Surely, we have been left indebted,

67. Rather, we have been left with nothing (we are completely deprived).'

Thinking Points

There are some important words that we must review in this section:

1. The word *'ḥuṭām'* means 'to break and crush something.'

2. The word *'tafakkahūn'* means 'to eat some fruit,' but it can also mean 'to speak foolish things, be in a state of amazement, or show remorse.'
3. The word *'mughramūn'* comes from the root *'gharāmah,'* and it means 'payment of damages and losses.'

When a person dies and is buried, the earth will transform that human body into dust – however, it is interesting to note that the seeds that we plant into the ground do not turn into dust or dirt. Instead, they have two opposite movements – the shoots grow and stretch into the sky, while the roots make their way deep into the ground. The roots absorb the nutrients in the soil, while the shoots break through any barriers, even if they are very rigid. Thus, one seed can transform into many clusters of whatever it is going to produce, and then it reproduces; whereas the human body decays and decomposes into 'nothing.'

Any type of transformation or change that "nature" goes through is the same for Allah ﷻ to carry out – as ultimately, He is the One overseeing all of these changes. Thus, life and death of various creatures; sweet or salty water, etc. – all are one and the same in their creation for Allah ﷻ. [By this we mean that there is no issue of "easy" or "hard"; "fast" or "slow" for Allah ﷻ – as some may think that one action is "easier" for Allah ﷻ to carry out than something else. – Tr.]

One of the ways to know things better is to study opposites, as the saying goes: 'We can know things and their importance by knowing their opposite.' For example, we know darkness through having light, we know sweet through experiencing sour, etc.

Looking around us and seeing all of the blessings that Allah ﷻ has given us – if either the night or day were longer than they are, or if the water of the Earth was to sink into the ground, or if all of the plants on Earth were to be thorny, or if all the water on Earth were to become undrinkable, and the list goes on – then who is there who could change that state for us, other than the One True God – Allah ﷻ?

Thus, if an individual was to pay attention to the crucial point that at any second, whatever they have from Allah ﷻ could easily be changed or even taken away from them, then they would actually think about the consequences of their actions. From this point, they would be in a better position to consider the worth of the blessings they currently have and could be drawn closer to the Grace and Power of Allah ﷻ.

Take Away Messages

1. That same Power that can produce clusters of food from one single seed can resurrect a human being from a single dead cell.
2. Actions and their natural reactions are all carried out by the Will of Allah ﷻ.
3. There are some people who, unless and until their actions take on a bitter outcome, do not have a wakeup call of their own conscience.

Part 12: Think About Your Water – Verses 68-70

أَفَرَءَيْتُمُ ٱلْمَآءَ ٱلَّذِى تَشْرَبُونَ ﴿٦٨﴾ ءَأَنتُمْ أَنزَلْتُمُوهُ مِنَ ٱلْمُزْنِ أَمْ نَحْنُ
ٱلْمُنزِلُونَ ﴿٦٩﴾ لَوْ نَشَآءُ جَعَلْنَٰهُ أُجَاجًا فَلَوْلَا تَشْكُرُونَ ﴿٧٠﴾

68. Have you seen (given thought to) the water that you drink?
69. Is it you who send it down from the clouds, or is it We who send it down?
70. If We Willed, We could make it bitter. Then why do you not give thanks?

Thinking Points

There are two words we need to focus on in this section:

1. The word *'muzn'* refers to 'the white clouds that bring rain.'
2. The word *'ujāja'* refers to 'bitter, salty water.'

We read in a *ḥadīth* that anytime the Messenger of Allah ﷺ would drink water, he would say: "All praise belongs to Allah, the One Who quenches our thirst with the sweet, potable water through His Mercy, and did not make it (water) salty or bitter, due to my sins."[74]

Different analyses such as focusing on the role of water in quenching a person's thirst *(tashrabūn)*, where the water comes from *(min al-muzni)*, the coming down of rain *(naḥnu munzilūn)*, and the taste of water *(low nashāʾ lajalnāhu ujājā)* should lead a person to be grateful to Allah ﷻ for all of these blessings.

We must always keep in mind that the continuous graces of Allah ﷻ are not an indication of His inability to change them. The unceasing blessings we receive from Allah ﷻ, such as health, sustenance, and guidance, are not due to His inability to withhold or alter them. Rather, they are a testament to His boundless mercy and patience. The capacity of Allah ﷻ to bestow and withdraw blessings is limitless; and He is fully able to change our circumstances in an instant if He Wills. However, in His infinite Wisdom, He often allows these graces to persist, even when humanity is ungrateful or heedless, as a sign of His immense forbearance and compassion. This continuity is meant to remind us of His never-ending generosity and give us an opportunity to recognize and appreciate His favours, rather than taking them for granted.

The endless kindness of Allah ﷻ is also a test of our character and faith. Just because Allah ﷻ continues to shower

---

[74] Barqī, Aḥmad ibn Muḥammad ibn Khālid al-, *Al-Maḥāsin*, Vol. 2, Pg. 449, Section 46, Ḥadīth 350:

أَلْحَمْدُ لِلَّهِ الَّذِي سَقَانَا عَذْبًا فُرَاتًا بِرَحْمَتِهِ وَلَمْ يَجْعَلْهُ مِلْحًا أُجَاجًا بِذَنْبِي.

us with blessings does not imply that He is unaware of our actions or unable to respond. Instead, He is giving us a chance to develop self-awareness, gratitude, and a sense of accountability.

The Quran frequently reminds us that blessings and hardships are both trials, designed to see who will turn to Allah ﷻ in gratitude and patience. If the Almighty were to withhold His blessings each time we faltered, then we would be left in constant deprivation. Instead, He overlooks many of our shortcomings, encouraging us to spiritually turn back to Him.

Therefore, the uninterrupted nature of Allah's Grace should inspire awe and humility in human beings, rather than complacency. It is a reminder that His Mercy far exceeds our understanding and is not a reflection of weakness or inability on His end. Recognizing that Allah ﷻ can change our circumstances at any moment encourages us to live with gratitude, humility, and a renewed commitment to our faith, making the most of the blessings He has granted us.

The portion of the verse which reads 'If We Willed' implies that Allah ﷻ did not make all of the water on Earth salty – although it is the majority of water. However, He is able to do so if He Wills, but again out of His Grace and Love for His creations, He Willed for the water to be nourishing and drinkable.

Lastly, paying attention to Divine favours not only strengthens the belief in Monotheism within a person, but it also revives the spirit of thanksgiving, while reconfirming the ability of Allah ﷻ to bring the dead back to life can also fortify our belief in the Almighty Creator.

Take Away Messages

1. The Quranic proofs are comprehensive and simple, yet at the same time they are profound – a glance at something like water is enough to draw a human being's attention to their original source of life – Allah ﷻ, and their end – the Resurrection.
2. The sending of potable water is a sign of Divine Wisdom and Power.
3. The sending down of rain from the skies is beyond the ability of any human being, and this is sufficient to recognize Allah ﷻ as the All-Powerful Creator of everything, and the fact that there is no action which takes place except by the Will of Allah ﷻ.
4. Studying the creations of various things can pave the way for showing gratitude, especially if one truly thinks and reflects upon these wonders of the universe.

Part 13: The Fire we Kindle – Verses 71-74

أَفَرَءَيْتُمُ ٱلنَّارَ ٱلَّتِي تُورُونَ ﴿٧١﴾ ءَأَنتُمْ أَنشَأْتُمْ شَجَرَتَهَآ أَمْ نَحْنُ
ٱلْمُنشِـُٔونَ ﴿٧٢﴾ نَحْنُ جَعَلْنَٰهَا تَذْكِرَةً وَمَتَٰعًا لِّلْمُقْوِينَ ﴿٧٣﴾ فَسَبِّحْ
بِٱسْمِ رَبِّكَ ٱلْعَظِيمِ ﴿٧٤﴾

71. Have you seen (given thought to) the fire which you kindle?

72. Is it you who produce the tree for (kindling) it (into fire) or are We the Producer (of it)?

73. We have made it a reminder (source of admonition for people), and provision for the wayfarers (travelers).

74. Therefore, glorify the Name of your Lord, the (Incomparably) All-Magnificent.

Thinking Points

Before we delve into the commentary, let us review a few key words:

1. The word *'tūrūn'* comes from the root word *'wa-ra-ya'* and refers to 'extracting something that was hidden;' and the word *'warā''* means 'the inside of something' or 'the back side of a thing.' When speaking about fire, and those things that are used to

further ignite a fire, or when using them to describe how the flames jump out, the term *‘īrā”* is used. In Ḥijāz (the Arabian Peninsula), there were two types of trees that were used in tandem with one another to start a fire – just like how people often use two rocks to light a fire by striking them against one another to create the spark.

2. The word *‘muqwīn’* comes from the word *‘qiwāyah,’* and it means ‘an open desert;’ and when speaking about ‘a person who travels through the desert’ the term *‘muqawwī’* is often used.

From verse 48 in which there was a show of doubt about the Resurrection and the Day of Judgement until this current verse under review, Allah ﷻ addresses humanity more than twenty times, and invites them to reflect on how things have come about, from their crops, water, and fire to the creation of themselves. The Almighty does this so that any doubts that people may have about Him being the Sole Creator can be removed from their minds.

In these few verses, the four elements: earth, water, wind, and fire have been spoken about, and how all of these are under the control and orders of Allah ﷻ. It is through the wonders and abilities of these things that we can come to recognize the Almighty Creator and realize His Power.

In addition, we see that in this chapter of the Quran, there are four instances in which Allah ﷻ questions people asking them, rhetorically, that if He did not have a direct hand to play in creating human beings, sending down rain, bringing forth vegetation, and creating fire – then who would be able to do all of these things for them!?

The requirement of fire, especially for those people living in the barren deserts, is something that is more needed than for those living in today's day and age in modernized societies in which we have little need for fire – as we cook using electric or gas stoves. However, in the past and even in some societies today, travelers in the desert need the heat and warmth offered by fire to protect themselves from the cold, to be able to find their way around during the dark nights, to ward off any wild animals while on their journey, and to prepare their food. Thus, Allah ﷻ makes mention of this important element.

Take Away Messages

1. The same Creator who allows fire to be kindled by and sustained by wood from a tree can also bring the dead who are buried deep in the ground back to life. This verse draws a comparison between the Power of Allah ﷻ to bring fire from wood, and His Power to resurrect the dead from the earth. Just as fire, hidden within the fibers of wood, can be ignited and emerge, the dead, who are buried in the earth, will be brought forth by the command of Allah ﷻ on the Day of Resurrection. These verses invite reflection on the immense abilities of the Almighty to transform and revive, emphasizing that He can initiate life after death just as He brings latent and dormant fire into existence.
2. The emergence of fire from a tree – which is used to create and sustain the fire – can remind a person of the Resurrection in two ways: first, the way the

release of stored energy manifests as sparks and eventually a fire; and second, how worldly fire serves as a reminder of the fire of Hell. On one level, this verse reflects the way hidden energy is released as a flame, symbolizing how life is resurrected after being concealed or dormant. On another level, earthly fire can prompt people to reflect on the reality of Hellfire in the Hereafter. The phrase "We have made it a reminder" emphasizes that such occurrences in nature are signs for humankind to remember spiritual truths, including the afterlife and accountability.

3. Allah ﷻ mentions everything that is required to remove any doubts about the belief in the Resurrection and the Day of Judgement from the minds of the people – whether it has an effect on them or not. Allah ﷻ then tells the Prophet ﷺ that his responsibility after all of this is simply to glorify Allah ﷻ.

Part 14: Oaths of Allah – Verses 75-76

فَلَآ أُقۡسِمُ بِمَوَٰقِعِ ٱلنُّجُومِ ﴿٧٥﴾ وَإِنَّهُۥ لَقَسَمٞ لَّوۡ تَعۡلَمُونَ عَظِيمٌ ﴿٧٦﴾

75. But nay, I swear by the setting of the stars.

76. And indeed, it is an oath – if you could only know – (most) great.

Thinking Points

There is nothing and no one who, without the permission of Allah ﷻ, can have any effect in this temporal world. Thus, the belief that the stars or any of the celestial bodies play a role in the destiny of an individual is nothing more than a superstition. No one has a 'lucky or unlucky star' in the sky that can affect a person's felicity or misfortune in this world. In light of this, Imam Mūsā ibn Jaʿfar al-Kāẓim ؏ said: "Allah praises the stars and takes an oath by their places in the sky."[75]

The phrase "by the setting of the stars," refers to "the location of the stars in the sky." Taking an oath by the celestial circle of movement of the stars is even more important than taking an oath by the stars themselves because the magnitude and vastness of the locations of the stars are thousands of times more in number than the number of stars themselves.

---

[75] *Tafsīr Rāhnumā.*

Take Away Messages

1. In this chapter, Allah ﷻ takes the intellect of a human being on a journey from the sperm and egg to a seed grown in the earth, to the water that we drink to the fire that we kindle. From there, He takes the human intellect on a journey of the movement of the celestial bodies in the sky.
2. Sometimes in the Quran, Allah ﷻ takes an oath by small things like the fig and the olive, and sometimes He takes an oath by the galaxy and the movements of the stars. For Allah ﷻ, "small and big" or a "fly and a mountain" are one and the same – it is only us who see things as being "small" or "big."
3. Every star has its own circuit and order – a specific path on which it runs.
4. Despite all efforts and scientific advancements, human beings still have not developed a comprehensive knowledge about the movements of all the celestial bodies in existence; and the Science of Astronomy and Human Cosmology is still an incomplete and ongoing science.

Part 15: The Noble Quran – Verses 77-80

إِنَّهُۥ لَقُرۡءَانٞ كَرِيمٞ ٧٧ فِي كِتَٰبٖ مَّكۡنُونٖ ٧٨ لَّا يَمَسُّهُۥٓ إِلَّا
ٱلۡمُطَهَّرُونَ ٧٩ تَنزِيلٞ مِّن رَّبِّ ٱلۡعَٰلَمِينَ ٨٠

77. Indeed, it is a Noble Quran,

78. In a Book well-preserved (in all of its purity).

79. None can touch it except those (who are) purified.

80. (It is) a revelation from the Lord of the Worlds.

Thinking Points

Apparently, the meaning of "A Book well-preserved" is that which is known as the *Lawḥ al-Maḥfūdh,* as can be seen in the Quran where we read: "Nay! It is a Glorious Quran, in a Preserved (Guarded) Tablet."[76]

In the Quran, Allah ﷻ normally refers to those things that are attributed to Himself with the word *'Karīm'* which means 'noble' or 'generous.'

The term *'karīm'* in the Quran encompasses both the basic meaning of 'generous' or 'noble,' and a deeper, multifaceted concept of goodness and honour. In its various forms, *'Karīm'*

---

[76] Quran, Sūrah al-Burūj (85), Verses 21-22:

﴿بَلۡ هُوَ قُرۡءَانٞ مَّجِيدٞ ٢١ فِي لَوۡحٖ مَّحۡفُوظِۭ ٢٢﴾

reflects Allah's ﷻ Attributes of Boundless Generosity, Noble Character, and Honourable Status. When referring to Allah ﷻ Himself, *'Karīm'* emphasizes His unlimited Kindness, Mercy, and Graciousness, showing that He bestows blessings without expectation, forgives readily, and honours His creations with dignity and mercy.

Beyond Allah's ﷻ nature, the term *'karīm'* also appears in other contexts in the Quran, highlighting characteristics of both people and objects. For example, it describes the Quran itself as a Noble Book, indicating its profound wisdom, dignity, and unmatched guidance. When used to describe the angels, *'karīm'* emphasizes their purity, reliability, and honourable role as the messengers of Allah ﷻ.

On a deeper level, *karīm* embodies not only generosity, but also a noble bearing and elevated status, emphasizing honour and dignity. Thus, *'karīm'* calls believers to embody these qualities by striving for moral excellence, humility, and generosity, showing that true honour is in the generous and noble character that Allah ﷻ embodies, and wishes for humanity to emulate.

We see this word used in the Quran in multiple ways, including the following:

1. **Allah ﷻ Himself:** "O humankind, what has deluded you concerning your Lord, the Generous?"[77]
2. **The Quran:** "Indeed, it is a Noble Quran."[78]

---

[77] Quran, Sūrah al-Infiṭār (82), Verse 6:

﴿يَٰٓأَيُّهَا ٱلۡإِنسَٰنُ مَا غَرَّكَ بِرَبِّكَ ٱلۡكَرِيمِ ٦﴾

[78] Quran, Sūrah al-Wāqiʿah (56), Verse 77:

3. **A Messenger Sent by Allah ﷻ:** "...And there came to them a Noble Messenger."[79]
4. **The Intermediary of the Revelation (Angel Jibrāʾīl ؑ):** "Verily, it (the Quran) is a Word (brought by) a noble (honourable) messenger (Angel Jibrāʾīl ؑ)."[80]

In addition, in Sermon 152 of *Nahj al-Balāgha*, Imam ʿAlī ؑ refers to the Ahlul Bayt ؑ as "The ennobled/dignified ones of the Quran."

Human beings have been referred to as being the best of creations of the Divine, and thus have been granted nobility (*kirāmah*): "And certainly, we have honoured the offspring of Ādam..."[81]

With respect to verse 79 of this chapter, it can be understood that it may be possible for everyone to read the words and understand the vocabulary of the Quran. However, a special level of purification is required in order to come into deeper and more spiritual contact with the heart

---

﴿إِنَّهُۥ لَقُرْءَانٌ كَرِيمٌ ۝٧٧﴾

[79] Quran, Sūrah al-Dukhān (44), Verse 17:

﴿...وَجَآءَهُمْ رَسُولٌ كَرِيمٌ ۝١٧﴾

[80] Quran, Sūrah al-Takwīr (81), Verse 19:

﴿إِنَّهُۥ لَقَوْلُ رَسُولٍ كَرِيمٍ ۝١٩﴾

[81] Quran, Sūrah al-Isrāʾ (17), Verse 70:

﴿وَلَقَدْ كَرَّمْنَا بَنِيٓ ءَادَمَ...۝٧٠﴾

and soul of the Words of Allah ﷻ, as the Quran says: "...Surely, Allah only desires to keep away the uncleanness from you, O people of the House, and to purify you with a (thorough) purification."[82]

We can see here in verse 79 of Sūrah al-Wāqiʿah, that Allah ﷻ did not say: "It (meaning the Quran) cannot be read, nor understood, except by those who are the purified ones."[83] Rather, He said: "None can touch it (achieve true insight into it) except those who are purified."

In this verse, the meaning of "touch" has a specific connotation – as we see in the traditions that: "It is only those who are near Allah who can 'touch' the Quran."[84]

With that said, the Quran is indeed Honoured and Noble *(Karīm)* because:

1. Its source is the Protected Tablet *(Lawḥ al-Maḥfūz)* and the Protected Book *(Kitāb al-Maknūn).*
2. The intermediaries who have received this Book: the angels, the final Messenger, Prophet Muḥammad ﷺ, and his Ahlul Bayt ؏ – are all spiritually pure.
3. The goal of this Book is to train and nurture all of humanity.

---

[82] Quran, Sūrah al-Aḥzāb (33), Verse 33:

﴿...إِنَّمَا يُرِيدُ ٱللَّهُ لِيُذْهِبَ عَنكُمُ ٱلرِّجْسَ أَهْلَ ٱلْبَيْتِ وَيُطَهِّرَكُمْ تَطْهِيرًا﴿٣٣﴾﴾

[83] What may be rendered as:

لَا يَقْرَئُهُ وَلَا يَفْهَمُهُ إِلَّا الْمُطَهَّرُونَ

[84] Suyutī, Jalāl al-Dīn, *Tafsīr Durr al-Manthūr.*

4. The Quran itself is pure, and it has "purified pages,"[85] and it is only those who are spiritually pure who can come into true contact with this Divine Book.
5. This Quran is not how its adversaries claim to be:
    a. Neither is it the thoughts nor imagination of the Prophet ﷺ that he dictated and his companions wrote down, passing it off as Divine Revelation: "...And they (the verses of the Quran) are dictated to him morning and evening."[86]
    b. Nor is it mythical legends as some people used to say (that he has taken the content of the Quran from previous scriptures and the stories passed down in other communities): "...This is nothing but mere tales of the ancients."[87]
    c. Neither is it a Book that Prophet Muḥammad ﷺ learned from others (as some historians

---

[85] Quran, Sūrah al-Bayyinah (98), Verse 2:

﴿رَسُولٌ مِّنَ ٱللَّهِ يَتْلُواْ صُحُفًا مُّطَهَّرَةً ۝٢﴾

[86] Quran, Sūrah al-Furqān (25), Verse 5:

﴿...فَهِيَ تُمْلَىٰ عَلَيْهِ بُكْرَةً وَأَصِيلًا ۝٥﴾

[87] Quran, Sūrah al-Anfāl (8), Verse 31:

﴿...إِنْ هَٰذَآ إِلَّآ أَسَٰطِيرُ ٱلْأَوَّلِينَ ۝٣١﴾

claim): "...A human being is teaching him (Muḥammad)..."[88]

d. Nor is the Quran the work of people that helped Prophet Muḥammad ﷺ: "...And other people have assisted him with it..."[89]

Rather, this Quran is a Book that has come from the Lord of the Universe, Allah ﷻ, for the advancement of humanity, as He clearly says: "(It is) a Revelation sent down from the Lord of the Worlds."[90]

The Quran is the key to esteem and honour for both an individual, as well as society. Looking at this Book, reciting it, thinking about its deep contents, memorizing the verses of it, using it as evidence, and taking lessons from its contents is the spring of spiritual growth and honour for an individual – because: "Indeed, it is a Noble Quran."

In issues related to an individual, a family, society, economy, politics, worship, military, ethical, theological, nurturing, and cultural, the Quran grants human beings light *(nūr)* and clarity because: "Indeed, it is a Noble Quran."

---

[88] Quran, Sūrah al-Naḥl (16), Verse 103:

﴿...إِنَّمَا يُعَلِّمُهُۥ... ١٠٣﴾

[89] Quran, Sūrah al-Furqān (25), Verse 4:

﴿...ٱفْتَرَىٰهُ وَأَعَانَهُۥ عَلَيْهِ قَوْمٌ ءَاخَرُونَ... ٤﴾

[90] Quran, Sūrah al-Ḥāqqah (69), Verse 43:

﴿تَنزِيلٌ مِّن رَّبِّ ٱلْعَٰلَمِينَ ٤٣﴾

There are no weak, ugly, imbalanced, or illogical statements in the Quran because: “Indeed, it is a Noble Quran.”

Take Away Messages

1. In speaking about the greatest document of legislation – meaning the Quran – Allah ﷻ takes an oath by the biggest of His creations, i.e. the galaxies.
2. The Quran, with all of its greatness, has offered its teachings to the entire world and all of humanity, and anyone can make use of its guidance.
3. The Quran is not merely words and phrases, but rather it possesses lofty content that is safeguarded and preserved by Allah ﷻ.
4. Utilizing the Quran requires a person to follow certain etiquette; those who are not in a state of spiritual purity such as with *wuḍū* (or other such acts legislated in Islam that offer purification to an individual) have no right to touch the wordings of it.
5. The deeper truths and realities of the Quran cannot be understood by those who are infected with polytheism, disbelief, hypocrisy, or obstinacy.
6. The Quran is a manifestation of the Lordship of Allah ﷻ, and it is a comprehensive plan for the growth and development of all human beings from the days of Prophet Muḥammad ﷺ until the end of times.

Part 16: How Can People Still Deny – Verses 81-82

أَفَبِهَٰذَا ٱلْحَدِيثِ أَنتُم مُّدْهِنُونَ ﴿٨١﴾ وَتَجْعَلُونَ رِزْقَكُمْ أَنَّكُمْ
تُكَذِّبُونَ ﴿٨٢﴾

81. Is it this (Divine) discourse [the Quran] that you are the deniers of?

82. And do you make the denial of it your job?

Thinking Points

Before we can review these two verses, let us have a look at one key word that Allah ﷻ uses in this section. The word *'mudhinūn'* comes from the word *'duhn'* and means 'oil;' while a word that comes from the same root word and is often used – *'mudāhinah'* – is sometimes used in the meaning of 'tolerance and leniency,' and sometimes it comes in the meaning of 'debility or weakness.' These meanings should be kept in mind when reading and reflecting on verse 81.

Once, the Noble Prophet of Islam ﷺ was with a group of individuals on a journey, and as their thirst began to grow, they realized that they were short of water. The Prophet ﷺ raised his hands in supplication, and thereafter it began to rain, quenching everyone's thirst. One of the individuals present said: "This rainfall is due to such and such star which has just risen (and not the supplication of the Prophet ﷺ)!" It was then that the following verse of the Quran was revealed: "And do you make the denial of it [Prophet Muḥammad ﷺ and his connection to Allah ﷻ] your job?"

The Prophet ﷺ then said to his travel companions: "Rather than thanking (Him) for your sustenance, you decide to deny Him!?"[91]

There are always individuals in society who see their own presence and character in opposition to others and use everything at their disposal to criticize other people. If a group of individuals agree on something, then they will oppose it; but if that same group are opposed to something, they will stand up in favour of it.

Such a person has no reason to justify why they carry out their actions in such a manner. Rather, they simply want to always defy and act contrary to how others act; and this is seen in their actions, words, and interactions with others. In all areas of life – even in things such as combing their hair or grooming their face, the colour and type of clothing they wear, the tone and style of speaking, the words and terminologies that they use when speaking to others or in their writings, and even when it comes to naming their children! Such individuals act in unconventional ways and like to draw attention towards themselves, and through this they want to make it seem like they are distinct and better than others.

---

[91] In this *ḥadīth*, Prophet Muḥammad ﷺ was referencing this verse of the Quran under review.

Take Away Messages

1. The more sacred and revered something is, the greater the possibility becomes of some people taking that thing lightly and not giving it the importance that it is entitled to. Due to this, they are at a greater level of being reprimanded.
2. Defiance and compromise in regard to the established religious principles is something that can never be accepted.
3. Negligence, idleness, and compromise in matters of religion will gradually lead a person to the field of denial of religion and the tenants of it – possibly making the individual leave religion in its totality.

Part 17: The Reality of Death – Verses 83-87

فَلَوْلَآ إِذَا بَلَغَتِ ٱلْحُلْقُومَ ﴿٨٣﴾ وَأَنتُمْ حِينَئِذٍ تَنظُرُونَ ﴿٨٤﴾ وَنَحْنُ أَقْرَبُ
إِلَيْهِ مِنكُمْ وَلَـٰكِن لَّا تُبْصِرُونَ ﴿٨٥﴾ فَلَوْلَآ إِن كُنتُمْ غَيْرَ
مَدِينِينَ ﴿٨٦﴾ تَرْجِعُونَهَآ إِن كُنتُمْ صَـٰدِقِينَ ﴿٨٧﴾

83. Why then, when the soul (of a dying person) reaches the throat,

84. And you are at that time looking on (helplessly),

85. And (when) We are nearer to them than you, but you do not see.

86. Why then, if you are not governed by any authority and are not to be requited,

87. You do not bring it (the soul) back (to the body of the dying person), if you are truthful (in your claim of being independent of the supreme Authority of Allah ﷻ)?

Thinking Points

If those who deny resurrection doubt the Power of Allah ﷻ in terms of Him being able to bring the dead back to life, then will they also deny the Power of Allah ﷻ in taking away the life of human beings as well?

Such deniers witness the scene in front of their very eyes in which a friend, a family member, or a loved one is on the verge of dying – and despite doctors or others being there doing all they can, they see that no one can do anything to stop this from happening. They experience their own powerlessness firsthand and witness the Power of Allah ﷻ at the time of impending death.

They must realize that the same Power that He must take away someone's life is the same Power that He has which can once again infuse life into a person after death – not only on the Day of Resurrection, but even before that if He Wills.

If death was something that was not under the control and determination of Allah ﷻ, and was something that happened by chance, then it should be possible to prevent it – however, it is not. Perhaps it may be delayed in certain circumstances, but it can never be ceased entirely.

Thus, those who deny the existence of a supreme Creator and Maintainer – Allah ﷻ – need to bring their evidence for His nonexistence.

In this chapter, time and time again, multiple proofs are brought forth by Allah ﷻ to prove His Existence and Power. For example, we see verses like: "Have you given thought to (the sperm drop, your life-germ) that you emit?" Or "Have you ever given thought to that which you sow?" In addition: "Have you given thought to the fire which you kindle?"

Of course, people should be humbled when they are shown the scenes of their own lives that they are completely incapable of doing anything about to change their situation in these glimpses of their pre-existence, just as we see in these verses in which Allah ﷻ speaks to them and says: Why, then, when the soul of a dying person reaches the throat, and you stand by there helplessly watching, unable to intervene – though I am nearer to them than you, yet you cannot perceive Me – if you truly believe you are beyond My Authority, then why do you not bring the soul back if you are truthful in your denial of My Power?

Allah ﷻ is close to all His servants – whether they are good or bad, as He says: "We are nearer to them." Therefore, what we must realize from such a verse is that what is important and carries value is that we, too, must seek to attain closeness to Allah ﷻ through our faith and righteous actions as He is always close to us.

The word *'madīn'* comes from the word *'dayn'* and means 'retribution.' Therefore, the phrase *'Yawm al-Dīn'* – which is one of the names of the Day of Judgement as we constantly read in Sūrah al-Fātiḥa and is normally translated as 'Master of the Day of Judgement' – is really the Day of Retribution or the Day of Payback – the Day when debts and everything else will come due.

Another thing that needs to be kept in mind before we close our review of this section is that 'looking' (*tanzurūn* - تَنْظُرُون) is not the same as 'seeing' (*tubṣirūn* - تُبْصِرُون) – how many times is it that a person 'looks' at something, however, cannot really 'see it' because one has become distracted with other things?

Take Away Messages

1. The last moments of dying, and death itself, are a surety for everyone. The word used in verse 83 which

is *'idhā'* comes when the thing being discussed is something that will definitely occur.

2. The exiting of the soul from the body will take place from the respiratory tract and the throat.
3. To resolve any hesitations that people may have regarding resurrection or the Day of Judgement, Allah ﷻ speaks about His Power during the period of one's life, as well as at the time when death is near, to ensure that He completes the proofs against the human being.
4. Allah ﷻ is the closest entity to a human being, closer than anyone else can ever be. The closeness that people have for one another is a physical proximity – however, the closeness that Allah ﷻ has with humanity stems from Him completely surrounding (metaphysically) His creations.
5. The Resurrection of human beings, and the punishments and rewards that will be awarded to everyone in the next life are definite. This can be understood by the usage of the past tense verb to describe an event that will transpire in the future – this means that something is definitely going to happen.

Part 18: Summary of Groups of People – Verses 88-96

فَأَمَّآ إِن كَانَ مِنَ ٱلۡمُقَرَّبِينَ ﴿٨٨﴾ فَرَوۡحٞ وَرَيۡحَانٞ وَجَنَّتُ نَعِيمٖ ﴿٨٩﴾
وَأَمَّآ إِن كَانَ مِنۡ أَصۡحَٰبِ ٱلۡيَمِينِ ﴿٩٠﴾ فَسَلَٰمٞ لَّكَ مِنۡ أَصۡحَٰبِ
ٱلۡيَمِينِ ﴿٩١﴾ وَأَمَّآ إِن كَانَ مِنَ ٱلۡمُكَذِّبِينَ ٱلضَّآلِّينَ ﴿٩٢﴾ فَنُزُلٞ مِّنۡ
حَمِيمٖ ﴿٩٣﴾ وَتَصۡلِيَةُ جَحِيمٍ ﴿٩٤﴾ إِنَّ هَٰذَا لَهُوَ حَقُّ ٱلۡيَقِينِ ﴿٩٥﴾ فَسَبِّحۡ
بِٱسۡمِ رَبِّكَ ٱلۡعَظِيمِ ﴿٩٦﴾

88. Then if the one (the departed person) belongs to those who have attained nearness (to Allah ﷻ and are among His chosen ones),
89. Then (they will have) happiness, comfort, and a garden of bliss.
90. And if the one (the departed person) belongs to the blessed people (Companions of the Right),
91. Then (it will be said to them): ‘Peace be upon you forever, (O you) from the blessed people!’
92. But if one belongs to those who denied the truth and are steeped in error,
93. Then (they will be offered) boiling water,

94. And will be burned in Hell.

95. Verily, this (fact) is the True Certainty,

96. Therefore, glorify the Name of your Lord, the All-Magnificent.

Thinking Points

There are a few words in this final section that we need to review before we can move on with the commentary:
1. The meaning of the word *'rawḥ'* is 'ease, comfort, and benevolence.'
2. The word *'rayḥān'* is used to refer to 'a sweet-smelling plant' and has also been used regarding 'sustenance' *(rizq).*
3. The word *'taṣliya'* comes from the root word *'ṣallā'* which means 'to taste something, to burn something, or to fall.'

At the beginning of this chapter, we read how people will be divided into three categories: "And (at that time) you shall be (sorted out into) three distinct categories." These were:
1. The people in close proximity to Allah *(al-Muqarrabīn).*
2. 'Companions of the Right' *(Aṣḥāb al-Yamīn).*
3. 'Companions of the Left' *(Aṣḥāb al-Shimāl).*

Now at the end of this chapter, we see that the outcome of these three groups is once again repeated.

Everyone will attain their rewards or punishments based on their own actions; just as Imam Jaʿfar al-Ṣādiq has been quoted as saying: "If a person who is on one's death bed happens to be of those in close proximity (to Allah), then *rawḥ* (ease and comfort) and *rayḥān* (a sweet-smelling plant) will be waiting for them in their grave, and Paradise will be full of blessings for them in the next life."

Of course, those in 'close proximity to Allah ﷻ' *(al-Muqarrabīn)*, by keeping in mind verses 10 and 11 of this chapter, are the pioneers in faith and righteous actions: "And the foremost will be the foremost (in the Hereafter); those are the ones brought near (to Allah)."

At the time of their death, the 'Companions of the Right' *(Aṣḥāb al-Yamīn)* will have their grief removed from them so that on the Day of Judgement, they will be able to attain their rewards.

Apparently, the meaning of '*Aṣḥāb al-Yamīn*' are those individuals who will be given their book of deeds in their right hand, and are the same people who have been spoken about in various other places in the Quran: "On the Day when We will call every (human) community with its leader; then whoever (has followed a leader towards true faith and righteousness, and belief in the Hereafter) will be given one's Record of Deeds (of life) in their right hand – those will read their book (with contentment), and they will not be wronged by even so much as a tiny hair."[92] As well: "Then, as for the one who is given the Record (of deeds) in one's right hand

[92] Quran, Sūrah al-Isrā' (17), Verse 71:

﴿يَوْمَ نَدْعُوا۟ كُلَّ أُنَاسٍۭ بِإِمَـٰمِهِمْ ۖ فَمَنْ أُوتِىَ كِتَـٰبَهُۥ بِيَمِينِهِۦ فَأُو۟لَـٰٓئِكَ يَقْرَءُونَ كِتَـٰبَهُمْ وَلَا يُظْلَمُونَ فَتِيلًا ٧١﴾

will say: 'Here, take and read my Record (Book of Deeds)!'"[93] Lastly, we see in the Quran: "Then, as for the one who will be given their Record in their right hand."[94]

As for the other group, the meaning of *'Aṣḥāb al-Shimāl'* (Companions of the Left) – are those people whose Book of Deeds will be given to them in their left hand. It has been mentioned in a tradition from Imam Muḥammad al-Bāqir that the meaning of those who are liars and misguided *(al-mukadhdhibīn wa al-ḍhāllīn)* are the polytheists.[95]

In regard to the portion of the verse that reads: "Then (it will be said to them): 'Peace be upon you forever, (O you) from the blessed people!'" – there are many interpretations for what this may mean, some of which include the following:

1. It will be said to the people of Paradise, without the mention of specific individuals: greetings be upon you.
2. The people of Paradise will send greetings upon the Prophet due to the troubles that he went through to help people reach the status they attained in Paradise.
3. The Prophet, due to the prosperity of this group of individuals, will find himself happy and in safety.[96]

---

[93] Quran, Sūrah al-Ḥāqqah (69), Verse 19:

﴿فَأَمَّا مَنۡ أُوتِيَ كِتَٰبَهُۥ بِيَمِينِهِۦ فَيَقُولُ هَآؤُمُ ٱقۡرَءُواْ كِتَٰبِيَهۡ ١٩﴾

[94] Quran, Sūrah al-Inshiqāq (84), Verse 7:

﴿فَأَمَّا مَنۡ أُوتِيَ كِتَٰبَهُۥ بِيَمِينِهِۦ ٧﴾

[95] *Tafsīr Nūr al-Thaqalayn.*

[96] *Tafsīr Rāhnumā.*

In verses 51 and 52, we read that: "Then, indeed you who have gone astray and are deniers (of the truth)! (You) will certainly eat from the trees of *zaqqūm*."[97]

However, in verses 92 and 93, we read: "But if one belongs to those who denied the truth and are steeped in error, then (they will be offered) boiling water."[98]

Why is it that in the first passage of verses (verse 51 in particular), the word *'ḍhāllīn'* precedes the word *'mukadhdhibīn,'* however, in the second passage of verses (verse 92 in particular), the opposite is the case?

The response to this is the following: It seems that in verse 51, the address is happening in this temporal world where a person who, due to their misguidedness, was pulled towards the denial of Allah ﷻ. However, at the end of the chapter in verse 92, the issue is focusing on the time of death of a person, which is the beginning of their punishment. Thus, contrary to the other verse, when it comes to punishment, it begins with that which is more difficult, and denial is weightier than deviation.

In these verses, the outcome of the three groups at the time of their death has been mentioned alongside one another so that in this spiritual showcase, an individual can be free to choose whichever path they please: "Then (they

---

[97] Quran, Sūrah al-Wāqiʿah (56), Verses 51-52:

﴿ثُمَّ إِنَّكُمْ أَيُّهَا ٱلضَّآلُّونَ ٱلْمُكَذِّبُونَ ۝٥١ لَآكِلُونَ مِن شَجَرٍ مِّن زَقُّومٍ ۝٥٢﴾

[98] Quran, Sūrah al-Wāqiʿah (56), Verses 92-93:

﴿وَأَمَّآ إِن كَانَ مِنَ ٱلْمُكَذِّبِينَ ٱلضَّآلِّينَ ۝٩٢ فَنُزُلٌ مِّنْ حَمِيمٍ ۝٩٣﴾

will have) happiness, comfort, and a garden of bliss ... Then (they will be offered) boiling water and burning in Hell."

There is no evidence brought forth when speaking about the rewards promised for those in proximity, and for the Companions of the Right. However, when it comes to retribution for the disbelievers, Allah ﷻ provides evidence for why they are deserving of such a severe punishment, and He states two things: They belied the truth, and were misguided individuals who did not seek to find true guidance in the life of this world.

Thus, we see that when it comes to reprimanding people, proof must be brought forth; however, when it comes to grace and love being shown, no one needs proof or reasons for why these are being conferred upon someone.[99]

Imam Jaʿfar al-Ṣādiq (ع) has been quoted as saying: "The welcoming [of the sinners] with boiling water will be done in the Intermediary Realm *(Barzakh)* in the grave; while entering into the fire of Hell will be after resurrection."[100]

In closing, this chapter began with a discussion about Resurrection and the Day of Judgement, and it also concludes with the mention of Resurrection and the Day of Judgement.

Take Away Messages

1. The Resurrection, the Day of Judgement, and the punishments and rewards in the next life are definite – and this can be verified by the usage of the past

---

[99] Rāzī, Fakhr al-Dīn al-, *Tafsīr al-Kabīr.*

[100] *Tafsīr Nūr al-Thaqalayn.*

tense verb to describe an event that will transpire in the future. This shows that something is going to happen.

2. For those near Allah ﷻ, death is merely the starting point of three unique forms of His Mercy:
    a. It is a way to part from the griefs and challenges of this temporal world *(rawḥ).*
    b. It is a path to attain the special Graces of Allah ﷻ *(rayḥān).*
    c. It is the means to secure perpetual success *(wa jannat naʿīm).*
3. Let us believe in, and take seriously, the moments of dying, death, and the accounts of how the souls of the close ones *(al-Muqarrabūn)*, the Companions of the Right *(Aṣḥāb al-Yamīn),* and the Companions of the Left *(Aṣḥāb al-Shimāl)* will depart.
4. The difficulties at the time of death that will be faced by the disbelievers, and their punishments with things such as the boiling water *(ḥamīm)* and the fire *(jaḥīm),* are all fair and just.
5. The punishment for a lifetime of deviancy and denial of Allah ﷻ is that those people will be welcomed into the next life with scalding drinks, and their eventual abode will be the burning fires. We must realize that Allah ﷻ is free from any kind of unfair forms of punishments, and these chastisements are all consequences of people's own actions.
6. Resurrection, the Day of Judgement, and the system of punishments and rewards are all signs of the Lordship of Allah ﷻ, and a means to help nurture and

train the human being – and this is something that all of humanity should praise the Almighty for.

Conclusion by the Translator

Sūrah al-Wāqiʿah, the 56th Chapter of the Quran, was revealed in Mecca, and has ninety-six verses.

Its primary theme was that of realizing the certainty and seriousness of the Day of Resurrection, thus, it is called *Al-Wāqiʿah* which means "The Inevitable Event".

It provides us with vivid scenes of the turmoil at the end of the world, and the destiny of humanity – emphasizing that the events foretold are not only possible, but inevitable due to the Omnipotence of Allah ﷻ.

This chapter opened by declaring the certainty of the Day of Resurrection, after which, we were confronted with the catastrophic upheavals that will precede that Day: The Earth being shaken, mountains being pulverized into dust, and how the natural order will collapse. This shocking transformation serves as both a warning and as assurance that no one can escape this reckoning. The use of the past tense to describe these future events which is a common Quranic rhetorical device highlights their inevitability and foregone nature, because for Allah ﷻ – these events are as good as done.

A characteristic of Sūrah al-Wāqiʿah is its detailed categorization of humanity into three distinct groups:

1. The Foremost *(al-Sābiqūn/al-Muqarrabīn)*: These are a select group described as being the closest to Allah ﷻ, excelling in faith and righteous deeds.
2. The Companions of the Right *(Aṣḥāb al-Yamīn)*: The righteous who will receive their book of deeds in their right hand, symbolizing salvation and entry into Paradise.

3. The Companions of the Left *(Aṣḥāb al-Shimāl)*: Those destined for perdition, who will receive their book of deeds in their left hand, so they are condemned to torment and punishment for their persistent sins and denial of truth.

The chapter elaborates at length on the rewards and states of the first two groups:

1. The Foremost, those brought nearest to Allah ﷻ, are described as reclining on ornamented thrones, served by immortal youths, and enjoying a Paradise of unending delights: pure drinks, fruits, riches, and companionship.
2. The Companions of the Right are also granted bliss, with references to lush shade, abundant fruit, flowing water, and perfect marital harmony.
3. In contrast, the Companions of the Left are shown enduring scorching wind, boiling water, and dark smoke – symbols of both physical and spiritual desolation. Their fate is linked to their arrogance, moral corruption, and denial of resurrection, presented as a logical consequence of their Earthly lifestyle.

Central to this chapter's argument for resurrection and accountability is a series of reflections on apparent worldly phenomena: the origin and development of human life from a drop of fluid, the growth of vegetation, the fall of rain, and the use of fire. Each natural process is invoked as a sign of Divine Power and Wisdom – serving not only as reminders of the wisdom of Allah ﷻ, but also as logical arguments for His ability to recreate and resurrect. The Quran challenges the reader and listener to consider whether they themselves control these processes, or if they are manifestations of a Higher Being. The recurrence of rhetorical questions: "Is it you who create... or are We the Creator?" reminds readers about the limits of human ability as well as knowledge.

We then transitioned to address the doubts harboured by skeptics regarding the resurrection. The chapter makes it clear that the decision of Allah ﷻ to bring about life, death, and ultimately a new creation is a calculated, purposeful act, not a series of aimless occurrence. The hidden wisdom behind life's cycle: birth, death, and succession of generations, demonstrates that worldly existence is a preparatory stage for the Hereafter and not the end.

Further, Sūrah al-Wāqiʿah emphasizes that the signs of Allah ﷻ are accessible to all levels of reflection: pondering the wonders of crops sprouting from the earth, the transformation and distribution of water, and the process of igniting fire from green trees. These moments offer not just gratitude for blessings, but also opportunities to cultivate deeper awareness of the Hereafter. This chapter weaves together these reminders to break any spiritual complacency and stir the intellect beyond ungratefulness or denial.

The Quran is also presented as noble and exalted: "A noble Quran, in a well-preserved Book" with its reality accessible only to those who are spiritually purified. This not only sets a high standard for approaching Divine revelation, but also signals the spiritual stakes involved in ignorance or heedless engagement with it. Allah ﷻ also reminds the readers that this Book is from the "Lord of the Worlds," countering any arguments that it is the product of human invention – Prophet Muḥammad ﷺ did not write the Quran!

In conclusion, this chapter returns to summarizing the fate of the three main human categories. It then closes with a call to glorify Allah ﷿, a return to the ultimate message that Divine Authority, Justice, and Mercy are the underlying foundation of all existence, accountability, and reward.

The discussion comes full circle: Sūrah al-Wāqiʿah begins and ends by situating human existence within an undeniable and purposeful cosmic order, where faith, gratitude, and righteous actions are both the standard and the means for enduring success.

May Allah ﷿ allow us to read, reflect, and implement the teachings of this profound chapter, Sūrah al-Wāqiʿah, allowing us to be within the first two groups which are spoken about.

الحمد لله رب العالمين

Other Publications Available[101]

1. *A Land Most Goodly: The Story of Yemen in the Quran and in the Times of Prophet Muḥammad and Imam ʿAlī ibn Abī Ṭālib,* by Jaffer Ladak
2. *A Star Amongst the Stars: The Life and Times of the Great Companion: Jabir ibn Abdullah al-Ansari,* by Jaffer Ladak*
3. *Alif, Baa, Taa of Kerbala,* by Saleem Bhimji and Arifa Hudda
4. *Arbāʿīn of Imam Ḥusayn,* compiled and translated by Saleem Bhimji
5. *Daily Devotions,* compiled and translated by Saleem Bhimji*
6. *Deficient? A Review of Sermon 80 from Nahj al-Balāgha,* by Āyatullāh al-ʿUẓmā Shaykh Nāṣir Makārim Shīrāzī and translated by Saleem Bhimji
7. *Exegesis of the 29th Juz of the Quran a Translation of Tafsīr Nemunah,* by Āyatullāh al-ʿUẓmā Shaykh Nāṣir Makārim Shīrāzī and translated by Saleem Bhimji*
8. *Foundations of Islamic Unity* a translation of *Al-Fuṣūl al-*

[101] The following is a list of all the original writings and translations from the Islamic Publishing House.

As many of these titles are out of stock, we are slowly re-releasing all our works via Print-on-Demand through Amazon.

Titles with an * after the name are currently available via Amazon from their international platforms, including Australia, Canada, France, Germany, Italy, Japan, UK, USA, Netherlands, and Spain.

If you cannot find any of the above titles on Amazon, feel free to email us at **iph@iph.ca**.

Muhimmah fī Ta'līf al-Ummah, by ʿAbd al-Ḥusayn Sharaf al-Dīn al-Mūsawī al-ʿĀmilī and translated by Batool Ispahany*

9. *Fountain of Paradise: Fāṭima az-Zahrā' in the Noble Quran,* by Āyatullāh al-ʿUẓmā Shaykh Nāṣir Makārim Shīrāzī, compiled and translated by Saleem Bhimji*
10. *God and god of Science,* by Syed Hasan Raza Jafri*
11. *House of Sorrows,* by Shaykh ʿAbbās al-Qummī and translated by Aejaz Ali Turab Husayn Husayni*
12. *Iʿtikāf: The Spiritual Retreat – The Philosophy, Spiritual Mysteries and Practical Rulings,* compiled and translated by Saleem Bhimji*
13. *Inspirational Insights,* by Mohammed Khaku
14. *Islam and Religious Pluralism,* by Āyatullāh Shaykh Murtaḍā Muṭahharī and translated by Sayyid Sulayman Ali Hasan
15. *Journey to Eternity – A Handbook of Supplications for the Soul,* compiled and translated by Saleem Bhimji and Arifa Hudda*
16. *Love and Hate for Allah's Sake,* by Mujtaba Saburi translated by Saleem Bhimji
17. *Love for the Family,* compiled and translated by Yasin T. Al-Jibouri, Saleem Bhimji, and others*
18. *Moral Management,* by Abbas Rahimi and translated by Saleem Bhimji*
19. *Morals of the Masumeen,* by Arifa Hudda
20. *Prayers of the Final Prophet – A Collection of Supplications of Prophet Muḥammad,* by ʿAllāmah Sayyid Muḥammad Ḥusayn Ṭabā'ṭabā'ī and translated by Tahir Ridha-Jaffer*
21. *Prospering Through a Cost of Living Crisis,* by Jaffer Ladak*

22. *Ramaḍān Reflections,* compiled by A Group of Muslim Scholars and translated by Saleem Bhimji*
23. *Ṣalāt al-Āyāt,* by Saleem Bhimji
24. *Ṣalāt al-Ghufaylah: Salvation through Patience & Perseverance,* written by Saleem Bhimji*
25. *Secrets of the Ḥajj,* by Āyatullāh al-ʿUẓmā Shaykh Ḥusayn Mazāherī and translated by Saleem Bhimji
26. *Sunan an-Nabī,* by ʿAllāmah Sayyid Muḥammad Ḥusayn Ṭabāʾṭabāʾī and translated by Tahir Ridha-Jaffer
27. *Tears from Heaven's Flowers: An Anthology of English Poetry about the Ahlulbayt,* by Abrahim al-Zubeidi
28. *The Day the Germs Caused Fitnah,* by Umm Maryam*
29. *The Firmest Armament: Commentary on Āyatul Kursī (The Verse of the Throne),* by Sayyid Nasrullah Burujerdi and translated by Saleem Bhimji*
30. *The Last Luminary and Ways to Delve into the Light,* by Sayyid Muḥammad Ridha Husayni Mutlaq and translated by Saleem Bhimji*
31. *The Muslim Legal Will Booklet,* by Saleem Bhimji*
32. *The Pure Life,* by Āyatullāh al-ʿUẓmā as-Sayyid Muḥammad Taqī al-Modarresī and translated by Jaffer Ladak with commentary by Dr. Zainali Panjwani and Jaffer Ladak*
33. *The Third Testimony: Imam ʿAlī in the Adhān,* compiled and translated by Saleem Bhimji*
34. *The Tragedy of Kerbalāʾ,* as narrated by Imam ʿAlī ibn al-Ḥusayn al-Sajjād, recorded by Shaykh al-Ṣadūq and translated by ʿAbdul Zahrāʾ ʿAbdul Ḥusayn*
35. *The Torch of Perpetual Guidance – A Brief Commentary on Ziyārat al-ʿĀshūrāʾ,* by ʿAbbās Azizi and translated by

Saleem Bhimji

36. *Weapon of the Believer,* by ʿAllāmah Muḥammad Bāqir Majlisī and translated by Saleem Bhimji*

Upcoming Publications

1. *Beyond the 40th: Understanding the Exclusive Significance of the Arbaʿīn of Imam al-Ḥusayn* ﷺ, by the late Āyatullāh al-Sayyid Muḥammad Muḥsin Ḥusaynī Ṭehrānī, translated by Saleem Bhimji
2. *Guided By Faith: The Islamic Management Model,* written by ʿAbbās Raḥīmī, translated by Saleem Bhimji
3. *Knocking on Heaven's Doors,* compiled with translations by Saleem Bhimji
4. *Propaganda and Piety: The Umayyad Rewriting of Syria [From Historical Syria to Apocalyptic Syria],* written by Dr. Rasūl Jaʿfariyān, translated by Saleem Bhimji
5. *Ramaḍān Devotions: A Collection of Supplications for the Nights of Qadr,* compiled with translations by Saleem Bhimji
6. *Blessed Desires: Islamic Perspectives on Sexuality and the Soul,* by ʿAlī Ḥoseinzādeh, translated by Saleem Bhimji
7. *Shadows of Dissent,* by Āyatullāh Shaykh Nāṣir Makārim Shīrāzī, translated by Saleem Bhimji and the Translator's Guild of the Islamic Publishing House
8. *Supplication for the People of the Frontiers,* by Shaykh Ḥusayn Anṣāriān, translated by Saleem Bhimji
9. *The Arbaʿīn: A look into the Ziyārat of Arbaʿīn,* written by Saleem Bhimji
10. *The Comprehensive Book of Marriage and Divorce Formulas,* by Saleem Bhimji
11. *The Young Muslims Daily Devotions Manuals – Volumes I and II,* compiled and translated by Saleem Bhimji
12. *Victor Not Victim: A Biography of Lady Zaynab binte ʿAlī*

and 200 Short Stories, researched and written by Saleem Bhimji

13. *Weekly Spiritual Ascent: Ṣalāt al-Jumuʿah: Philosophy, Practice, and Personal Piety*, compiled and translated by Saleem Bhimji

Our *Living the Quran Through The Living Quran* series of commentary on the Noble Quran is also being published. To date, we have released the commentary of:

1. Sūrah al-Fātiḥa (1)
2. Sūrah Yāsīn (36)
3. Sūrah Qāf (50)
4. Sūrah al-Najm (53)
5. Sūrah al-Wāqiʿah (56)
6. Sūrah al-Mujādilah (58)

The commentary of the following chapters of the Quran will also be released in the future:

1. Sūrah al-Ṣaff (61)

Supporting Our Projects

If you would like to donate to any of our ongoing projects, such as our upcoming book publications, video content, or article, you can contribute in the following ways:

Within Canada: Send an e-transfer from your Canadian bank account to **iph@iph.ca**

International: Send your transfer via PayPal to **saleem1176@rogers.com**

For more information,
check out our website:

www.iph.ca

Contact us for more information at:

iph@iph.ca

www.ingramcontent.com/pod-product-compliance
Lightning Source LLC
Chambersburg PA
CBHW031649040426
42453CB00006B/252